HOCPP 1002　　　　　　Teac

In the Hands of a Child

Grades 2 - 6

Project Pack
Butterflies

**A Ready-to-Assemble
Hands-On Unit
Including Reproducibles**

Thank you for your purchase from
In the Hands of a Child
Your Premiere Lapbook Provider since 2002!!

Butterflies
HOCPP 1002
Published: September, 2007

Authors:
Katie Kubesh
Niki McNeil
Kimm Bellotto

For information about other products available from In the Hands of a Child
Call 1-866-426-3701 or visit our website at www.handsofachild.com.

Entire contents of this Project Pack © 2007
In the Hands of a Child.
6222 Pierce Street
Coloma, MI 49038

Permission is hereby granted to the individual purchaser to reproduce student materials in this project pack for noncommercial individual or classroom use only. In the Hands of a Child gives permission for one copy of all written material to be copied and or printed. Classroom teachers have permission to reproduce one copy for each student in class. Members of co-ops or workshops have permission to reproduce one copy for up to 10 children per unit. Reproducible graphics may be reprinted as many times as needed. Permission is not granted for school wide or system wide reproduction of materials.
Printed in the USA.

Bringing Laughter and Learning Together
In the Hands of a Child

From the day we first began using and creating Project Packs we fell in love with them. We knew that this type of hands-on learning experience was just the thing that was needed to make boring unit studies not only educational but fun and exciting too!

To help you get started with your Project Pack, we have included some of the most frequently asked questions we receive about our Project Packs.

What is a Project Pack?
A Project Pack contains both the activities and the lesson plans or research guide needed to complete the activities. Imagine your child not only learning about the life cycle of a butterfly, but also creating a cocoon of his or her own. Students don't just read the story, *Blueberry Sal* by Robert McCloskey- they enjoy a "blue day" complete with a recipe for blueberry pancakes, making a "blue" collage, and don't forget painting a "blue" picture!

Why is this a better way to learn? How does this help me?
Student learning improves when lessons incorporate hands-on projects or crafts. Children learn by doing. Project Packs put learning into their hands! The possibilities are endless when your student begins a lapbook with a Project Pack from In the Hands of a Child. There are no age or skill limits and any topic or subject can be worked into a Project Pack.

When you purchase a Project Pack from In the Hands of a Child, all the work is done for you-the parent/teacher, but not for the student. In addition, Project Packs are easy to store, are an instant review tool, scrapbook, and a ready-made portfolio of all your student's studies.

How do I make a Project Pack?
A Project Pack is simply a file folder refolded into a shutter-style book. Open a file folder flat, fold each side into the middle and crease the fold neatly. There you have it!

What supplies do I need?
You need file folders, paper in different colors and weights*, your student's favorite coloring tools, tape, glue, scissors, and a stapler.

*For a more colorful and appealing Project Pack, it is suggested you print some of the reproducible graphics on colorful, multi-purpose paper. We recommend 24# weight or cardstock.

I have a Project Pack, NOW what?

We hope you are delighted with your new purchase, we'd like to share a few tips with you that we've found beneficial to other customers.
Here is a brief introduction to our product layout.

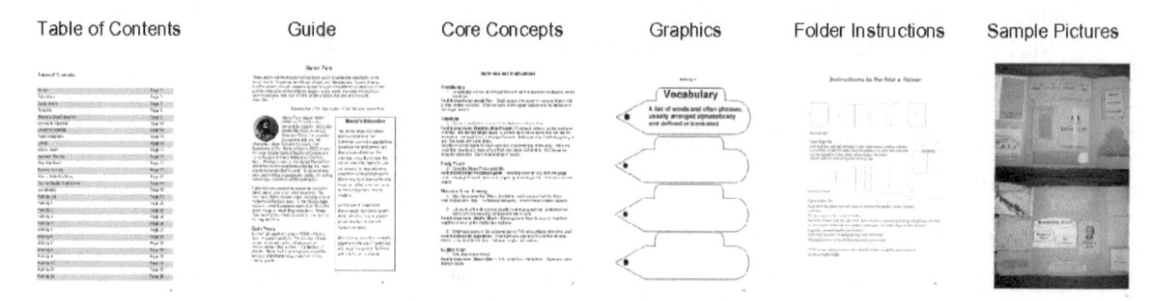

| Table of Contents | Guide | Core Concepts | Graphics | Folder Instructions | Sample Pictures |

Each unit starts with a Table of Contents and is followed by a Research Guide. The Research Guide contains all of the lessons needed to complete the activities laid out in a chapter-like format. This format helps to build students' listening, reading, and comprehension skills. Included in the Research Guide is a Bibliography, which also makes a great resource for finding information for any rabbit trails you may choose to follow during your study. Related books and websites are included in the Research Guide.

Next, you will find a list of core concepts to be covered during the study, each of the concepts is represented by a graphic organizer or template. Each graphic organizer or template helps students take bite-sized pieces of information learned in the Research Guide and complete a hands-on activity to help retain that information. If you implement graded assignments in your curriculum the list of concepts will be essential for you, the parent/teacher, to know what to test the student on. Under each concept you will find the folding instructions for each of the graphic organizers or templates. Each one has a corresponding activity number to make following along easy.

Reproducible graphics for the graphic organizers and templates follow. You may want to make a copy of each graphic for each student completing the unit. An instruction sheet for folding file folders and photos of sample lapbooks are included in the back section of each Project Pack. If you and your students are visual learners you will find the folder instructions and sample photos quite helpful.

Project Packs from In the Hands of a Child make great stand-alone unit studies or can easily be added as a supplement to an existing curriculum. When using as a stand-alone product we recommend completing 2 - 3 activities per session (30 - 45 minutes). Start out by reading through 2 - 3 sections of the Research Guide and then complete the corresponding hands-on activities. The hands-on activities correlate to each section in the Research Guide.

Vocabulary and Timeline activities do not have to be completed in one day. Vocabulary words can be learned throughout the entire study. We recommend that your student learn a few new vocabulary words each day or learn them as they are written in the Research Guide (all words in bold are vocabulary words). We also recommend Timeline activities be completed a little each day. Choose the vocabulary words and time periods you are going to add to your vocabulary books and timelines as you read them in the Research Guide.

If you are working with young children or a group of children, cut out all of the graphics a day or two before beginning the lapbook and store them in a zip-top bag. It is also helpful to have all materials organized before beginning. All of our early childhood Project Packs include a full supplies list on one of the very first pages!

Your student's completed Project Pack does not have to look like the photo featured at the end of the Pack. The photo is simply a reference to help you understand the folds and the process of putting the file folder together. If you run out of room or things do not fit, add another file folder or an extension! Allow children to take an active role in designing the layout of their project so that it becomes personal for them. The personalizing of their projects aids in the reinforcement of the study.

Your students may choose to attach the various activities to their folders as each one is completed or they may choose to wait until all activities are completed and then attach them to the file folder. If you choose to do the latter, simply store the activities in a zip-top bag, expandable file, or folder until you are ready to assemble them in a file folder.

Should you have any questions as you go about your study please do not hesitate to contact us, we are here to help you bring laughter and learning together in the Hands of Your Child!!

Niki, Kimm, and Katie
www.HandsofaChild.com

Niki can be reached at Niki@HandsofaChild.com or 1-866-HANDS-01
Kimm can be reached at Kimm@HandsofaChild.com
Katie can be reached at Katie@HandsofaChild.com

Adapting a Project Pack to Fit the Needs of Your Student

Adapting a Project or Research Pack is key to ensuring that you provide the best lesson for your student. At first glance, some might just skip over an activity because they feel it is too easy or too difficult for their student. We want you to use all the activities we provide…they are easily adaptable!

For example, if you have a PK-3 student the vocabulary activities might be difficult for him or her to complete. Here are some tips to help you adapt the activities that require your student to write:

1. Have your student dictate vocabulary words and their meanings as you write them.
2. Have your child draw a picture instead of writing.
3. You write the word or sentence first so your student can see how it is written (many of our Project Packs also include activities with dotted lines for easy copy work).
4. Practice. Practice. Practice. In the car, on a walk, in the shopping cart! Practice saying the vocabulary words and what they mean. Before you know it your preschooler will be telling others what those words mean!
5. Contact us. We would be happy to give you ideas for adapting specific units to a grade level.

On the other hand, some of the activities may seem too easy for your student. Does your 5th grade level student want to learn about butterflies, but the Project Pack seems too easy? Try it anyway; just change things up a bit to suit your student's grade level and skill. Here are some tips to help you adapt the activities to make them a little more difficult:

1. In addition to writing down vocabulary words and their meanings, ask your student to use the word in a sentence; either verbally or written.
2. Give your student one hour (or reasonable time frame) to research the topic on his or her own either online or at the library. Give your student a set of questions and see what he or she can find without your guidance.
3. Encourage your student to expand on the topic or choose a related subject to learn about.
4. Take a look at some of our preschool units…there is a lot of clipart related to each topic included. Have an older student cut these out and write a story or play about the pictures.
5. Contact us. We would be happy to give you ideas for adapting specific units to a grade level.

These are just few ways you can adapt a Project Pack to meet the needs of your student. Let your student be the judge if something is too easy or too difficult…you just might be surprised!

The Website links we have included in our guides are references we found that contain relevant information. However, the sites are not owned or maintained by In the Hands of a Child. The content may have changed or become a "dead" link. If you find the site contains inappropriate material or is no longer a relevant site, please let us know. Thank you.

Educator Notes:

Table of Contents

Planning Guide	Page 9
Related Reading	Page 11
Bibliography	Page 12
Activity Instructions	Page 13
Folder Instructions	Page 17
Sample Picture	Page 18
Research Guide	Page 20
Anatomy	Page 20
Range and Habitat	Page 22
Diet	Page 23
Pollination	Page 23
Life Cycle	Page 24
Caterpillars	Page 24
Predators and Defense	Page 26
Hibernation and Migration	Page 27
Butterfly or Moth	Page 28
Collecting and Gardening	Page 28
Conservation	Page 30
Vocabulary	Page 32
Reproducibles	Page 33
Answer Key	Page 83

	Vocabulary Words	**Guide Reading**	**Complete Activities**	**Continue Activities**
Day 1	Thorax Abdomen Compound eye Proboscis	Butterflies Butterfly Anatomy	2 – Butterfly Anatomy 3 – Proboscis Painting	1 - Vocabulary
Day 2	Antennae	Butterfly Anatomy *Monarch Butterfly	4 – Compound Eyes 5 – My Eyes	1 - Vocabulary
Day 3	Exoskeleton	*Exoskeleton Range and Habitat Temperate, Mountain, Tropical Butterflies	6 – Exoskeletons 7 – Butterfly Habitats	1 - Vocabulary
Day 4	Carnivorous	Diet *Buckeye Butterfly	8 – Butterfly Diet 9 – Drink Like a Butterfly	1 - Vocabulary
Day 5	Pollination Pollen	Pollination *Tiger Swallowtail Butterfly	10 – Pollination Activity: Coffee Filter Butterflies	1 - Vocabulary
Day 6	Caterpillar Larva	Life Cycle – Egg Stage	12 – Butterfly Eggs 14 – My Butterfly Eggs	1 - Vocabulary
Day 7	Silk Cocoon Pupa Chrysalis Metamorphosis	*Caterpillars Life Cycle – Larva/Caterpillar, Pupa, Adult *2 Cor. 5:17	11 – Butterfly Life Cycle 13 – My Cocoon	1 – Vocabulary

Have student complete vocabulary words slotted for each day from activity 1, then read the sections of the guide slotted for the day and any extra books you have on the topic. Finish up each day by having them complete the activities scheduled for that day.
NOTE: Items marked with a * are in text-boxed areas in the guide.

Day 8	Camouflage Mimicry Defense mechanism	Predators and Defense Defense Mechanisms	15 – Predators 16 – Defense Mechanisms	1 – Vocabulary
Day 9	Migration Predator	Hibernation and Migration *Did You Know?	17 – Baby, It's Cold Outside! 18 – Butterfly Migration	1 – Vocabulary
Day 10	Order	Is It a Butterfly or a Moth?	19 – Butterfly or Moth?	1 – Vocabulary
Day 11		Butterfly Collecting and Gardening	20 – Butterfly Collecting and Gardening 21 – My Butterfly Garden	1 – Vocabulary
Day 12	Conservation	Conservation *Extinction and Conservation	22 – Butterfly Info Card 23 – Protecting the Butterflies 24 – Butterfly Bookmark	1 – Vocabulary

Have student complete vocabulary words slotted for each day from activity 1, then read the sections of the guide slotted for the day and any extra books you have on the topic. Finish up each day by having them complete the activities scheduled for that day.
NOTE: Items marked with a * are in text-boxed areas in the guide.

Related Books and Websites

An Extraordinary Life: The Story of a Monarch Butterfly by Laurence P. Pringle
Attracting Birds, Butterflies, and Other Backyard Wildlife by David Mizejewski
Audubon's Butterflies, Moths, and Other Studies by Alice Elizabeth Ford
Butterfly Alphabet Book by Brian Cassie
Butterfly Colors by Helen Frost
Butterfly House by Eve Bunting
Butterflies by Donna Bailey
Charlie the Caterpillar by Dom DeLuise
Chasing Monarchs: Migrating With Butterflies of Passage by Robert Michael Pyle
Discover Butterflies by Gary Dunu
Do Monkeys Tweet? by Melanie Walsh
From Caterpillar to Butterfly by Deborah Heiligman
How Caterpillars Turn Into Butterflies by Jill Bailey
How to Raise Butterflies by E.J. Norsgaard
I Wish I Were A Butterfly by James Howe
Monarch Butterfly by Gail Gibbons
Miss Emma's Wild Garden by Anna Grossnickle Hines
National Audubon Society Field Guide to North American Butterflies by Robert Michael Pyle
Remember the Butterflies by Anna Grossnickle Hines
Strawberry Shortcake and the Butterfly Garden by Kelli Curry
The Art of the Butterfly by Ed Marquand
The Butterfly Alphabet Book by Brian Cassie and Jerry Pallotta
The Caterpillar and the Polliwog by Jack Kent
The Eyewitness Handbook of Butterflies and Moths by David Carter
The Lamb and The Butterfly by Arnold Sundgaard
The Magic School Bus Chapter Book: Butterfly Battle by Nancy White
The Very Hungry Caterpillar by Eric Carle
Waiting For Wings by Lois Ehlert
Where Butterflies Grow by Joanne Ryder

http://www.monarchwatch.org/
http://www.enchantedlearning.com/subjects/butterfly/
http://www.ca.uky.edu/entomology/entfacts/ef006.asp

Bibliography

Boring, Mel. *Caterpillars, Bugs, and Butterflies.* Minnesota: NorthWord Press, 1996.

Norsgaard, E. Jaediker. *Butterflies for Kids.* Minnesota: NorthWord Press, 1998.

Whalley, Paul. *Butterfly and Moth.* New York: Alfred A. Knopf, 1988.

http://bsi.montana.edu/web/kidsbutterfly/

http://centralamerica.com/cr/butterfly/

Butterfly Activities and Instructions

Vocabulary
1. Vocabulary: As you work through this unit, learn a few new vocabulary words each day.

Fold Instructions: *Pocket Book with Cards*- Fold the bottom section of the pocket book up to create the pocket, seal on the edges. Fold book in half so cover is on front. Store cards in pocket. Cut and paste definitions have been provided for younger students.

Butterfly Anatomy
2. Identify the parts of a butterfly.

Fold Instructions: *Stick Puppets*- Attach each butterfly graphic to a craft stick. Cut out the labels and attach one to each of the craft sticks on the backside of where the butterfly is attached. Have student color the correct part of the butterfly. They can then use the puppets as a self-checking system for anatomy identification.

3. Do you have a Proboscis?

Fold Instructions: *Large Butterfly Graphic*- Give each child a sheet of wax paper and one straw. Take a few colors of paint and water them down with equal parts of water and paint. Take a plastic spoon and draw a few blobs of paint onto the wax paper. The student is now ready to test their new proboscis (the straw) to blow the paint around the paper. Note: Be sure to instruct student not to suck in! Add as much or as little paint as desired and once they feel it is complete they will stick another piece of wax paper over the top to seal it their painting. Now take 2 copies of the graphic and cut out the sections of the wings on both copies. Sandwich the wax paper painting between the two copies of the graphic so the painting becomes the butterfly's wing sections. Trim away any excess wax paper.

4. How does a butterfly see? Explain what compound eyes are.

Fold Instructions: *Drawing Grid*- A butterfly would only see one square of the grid at a time. Practice seeing like a butterfly and draw only one square at time to create a complete butterfly.

5. How do your eyes see?

Fold Instructions: *Minibook*- Cut out the pages of the minibook and stack and staple on the left edge. See how well you can read the chart from different distances. Record your findings in your minibook.

6. What is an exoskeleton?

Fold Instructions: *Card book*- Fold the graphic half like a greeting card. Inside describe what an exoskeleton is what its purpose is.

Range and Habitat
7. List and describe the 3 main types of habitats that butterflies live in.
Fold Instructions: *Three-Door Book*- Cut on the dotted lines. Fold the flaps over on the solid line so that it forms three flaps. Write the title on the covers of the flaps or use the title blocks provided. Inside describe each of the main types of habitats butterflies live in. Cut and paste tracer options are included for younger students.

Diet
8. A Butterfly's Diet
Fold Instructions: *Shape Book*- Stack the pages of the book together and staple at the top edge. Inside describe the diet of a butterfly. Tracer pages have been provided for younger students.

9. Drink like a butterfly
Activity Instructions: *No Graphic*- You will need 3 clear cups, crushed ice, bright colored juice, a straw, and measuring cups. Fill one cup with crushed ice, add the juice to the ice, adding more ice if needed. Explain that butterflies will drink liquid from sand and mud. Have them pretend that the ice is the sand/mud and the juice is the water. Have them drink from one cup. Now repeat the procedure again except measure how much liquid you put into the ice. As the student sucks out the liquid, instruct them NOT to swallow it but to then blow it into the empty cup or measuring cup. Have them continue until they have gotten as much liquid as possible out. Did they take out as much as they put in? Why or why not?

Pollination
10. Sequence of Pollination
Fold Instructions: *Pocket Book with Cards*- Fold the bottom section of the pocket book up to create the pocket, seal on the edges. Fold book in half so cover is on front. Have students sequence the cards. Older students can write on the back of the cards about each stage of the pollination process. Store cards in pocket.

Life Cycle
11. Life Cycle Wheel
Fold Instructions: *Wheel-* Cut out the empty section of the top of the wheel. Place a brad through the black circle in the middle of both sections. Have students label each section to the right of the graphic.

12. How many eggs will hatch?
Fold Instructions: *Matchbook-* Cut out the main graphic and fold matchbook style. Paste the grid inside. Label each square 1 to 100. Have student color one square to represent each egg that will hatch.

13. Make your own butterfly cocoon
Activity Instructions: *No Graphic-* You will need scissors, white glue, warm water, a plastic disposable bowl, newspaper cut into strips, a long narrow balloon, and some paint. Blow up the balloon; mix 2 parts glue with 1 part warm water. Have student dip the paper into the glue mixture and cover the balloon in it. Continue to do this for several layers and then allow it to dry. Paint after it has completely dried. Create a dramatic display by collecting a stick from the outdoors to hang your cocoon on and add some pipe cleaner s to the butterfly made in previous activity and make it appear to emerge from the cocoon.

14. Make your own butterfly egg
Activity Instructions: *No Graphic-* You will need scissors, white glue, warm water, a plastic disposable bowl, newspaper cut into strips, a round balloon, and some paint. Blow up the balloon; mix 2 parts glue with 1 part warm water. Have student dip the paper into the glue mixture and cover the balloon in it. Continue to do this for several layers and then allow it to dry. Paint after it has completely dried.

Predators and Defense
15. List the main predators of butterflies
Fold Instructions: *Fan Book-* Stack the fans together and place a brad through the black circle on the end. Three options are provided depending on students writing ability, choose the one that fits your specific student's needs or skill level.

16. What defense mechanisms do butterflies use to protect themselves?
Fold Instructions: *Flap Book-* Can you see the three butterflies on the picture? It is difficult to see them because they are camouflaged! Cut out the three flap butterflies and fold the flaps over so they bend to the back of the picture and allow each of the butterflies to line up with those hidden in the picture. On the back of the flap butterflies list each of the defense mechanisms of a butterfly. Cut and paste words are provided for younger students.

Hibernation and Migration
17. List two different ways that butterflies survive a cold winter climate
Fold Instructions: *Concept book-* Cut on the dotted line and fold the two flaps that are formed up on the sold line. Under each flap describe each method butterflies use to survive in winter. Attach the title blocks to the cover of the flaps.

18. Map the migration path of butterflies
Fold Instructions: *Info Card-* Inside the info card glue the map. On the map add the migration path of butterflies. Fold the info card in half so cover is one top.

Is it a Butterfly or a Moth?
    19. Compare a butterfly to a moth

Fold Instructions: *Shaped Venn*- On the Venn diagram compare a butterfly to a moth. A tracer font graphic has been provided for younger students. Have younger students draw pictures to represent the differences next to the tracer font if they have the ability.

Butterfly Collecting and Gardening
    20. How does butterfly collecting and gardening help butterflies?

Fold Instructions: *Accordion Book*- Fold the graphic accordion style. Inside describe how butterfly collecting and gardening is helpful to butterflies. A tracer font option has been provided for younger students.

    21. Design a butterfly garden. What flowers will you plant?

Fold Instructions: *Info Card*- Fold the graphic in half. Inside draw your garden on the bottom of the card. On the top section create a key for your garden.

    22. Create an information card about a specific type of butterfly

Fold Instructions: *Card*- On the card describe the type of butterfly you selected.

Conservation
    23. How can you help protect butterflies?

Fold Instructions: *Minibook*- Stack and staple the pages on the left edge. Inside describe what you can do to help protect butterflies.

    24. Create a butterfly bookmark

Fold Instructions: *Bookmark*- Design your own bookmark.

Creating a Lapbook Base

Basic Lapbook Base
- Open a file folder and lay it flat.
- Fold both right and left edges toward the center so they meet and close like a pair of shutters.
- Crease firmly.

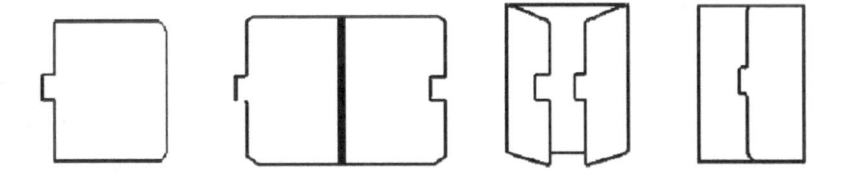

Base with Single or Double Extensions
- Complete the basic lapbook base.
- Open base and lay flat.
- Cut another folder in half or use a sheet of cardstock for the extension.
- Lay the extension in the center of folder at either the top or bottom. (You may add two extensions if need be; one at the top and one at the bottom).
- Attach to base with clear packing tape.

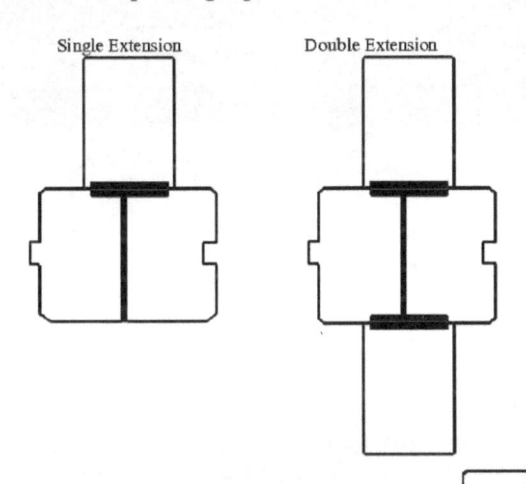

Double Folder Base
- Make two base folders.
- Open them and lay them side by side with outer flaps pointing straight up, not flat.
- Where the two flaps meet glue them together.
- Fold center flap to one side, fold both shutters in and close folders like a book.

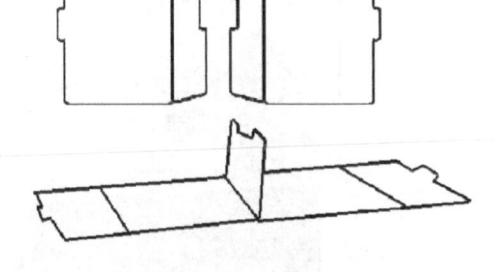

18 | Page

19 | Page

Butterflies

May the wings of the butterfly kiss the sun
And find your shoulder to light on,
To bring you luck, happiness and riches
Today, tomorrow, and beyond.
~Irish Blessing

How much butter could a butterfly fly if a butterfly could fly butter? Well, actually, butterflies don't fly butter at all! And if they could, they would not be able to fly very much of it since butterflies are very lightweight creatures! Butterflies are colorful insects that could be the most popular and easiest insects to recognize. There are about 20,000 different kinds of butterflies all over the world.

Butterfly Anatomy

Just like other insects, butterflies have six jointed legs and three body parts; the head, the **thorax**, and the **abdomen**. Butterflies also have **compound** eyes, a pair of antennae, and a long tube-shaped tongue called a **proboscis**.

Head

The head is in the front of the butterfly. This is where the antennae, the eyes, and the mouth are located.

- Antennae: A butterfly has two **antennae** on its head. They are long and thin with a small ball-shaped end. The antennae work like a human's nose, sniffing things out like nectar, flowers, and other butterflies!
- Compound Eyes: Butterflies have bulging compound eyes. They are made up of many tiny units like a bunch of little eyes all grouped together. Each unit sees a small part of what the butterfly is looking at. The butterfly's brain puts all the small pieces together to form one larger image. Compound eyes are good for seeing objects and motions to the side and almost to the back of the butterfly. They are not good for seeing things far away! For a butterfly, things that are far away are just a big blur.
- Mouth: Butterflies have long, skinny, curled-up tubes in the middle of their mouths. This tube is called a proboscis. The proboscis is made of two tubes that are like straws and the butterfly uses them to drink the nectar from flowers. When the butterfly is not using its proboscis for drinking, it keeps it curled up inside its mouth.

Thorax
The thorax is the middle part of the body and contains strong muscles that move the wings and legs. The thorax has three segments with one pair of legs attached to each one.

- Legs: The six jointed legs of a butterfly have a very special job. The legs are the part of the butterfly that has the sense of taste! Butterflies use their legs to find sweet tasting nectar to drink.

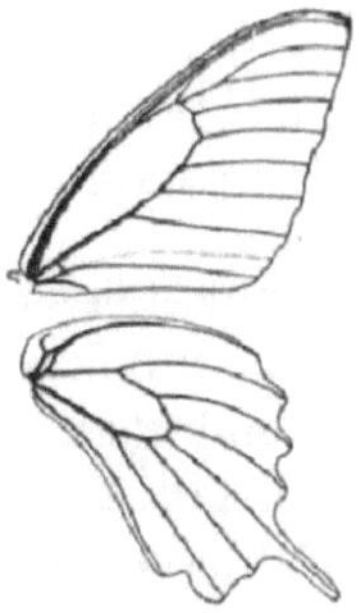

- Wings: Butterflies have four scaly wings; two forewings and two hindwings. The scales on their wings give them their beautiful colors. The colors of a butterfly's wings have a very important purpose. In the insect world, things that are brightly colored usually have a yucky taste or are poisonous! When predators see colorful insects, including butterflies, they do not try to eat them because they think it will not taste good or worse yet - will poison them! As butterflies age, their wings become worn and frayed and their colors begin to fade. This can be very dangerous for a butterfly.

Abdomen
The abdomen of the butterfly is soft and flexible. This part of the body has ten segments. On the sides of the abdomen are two holes. These holes are used to breathe in oxygen. The heart and the stomach of the butterfly are both in the abdomen.

Exoskeleton

Butterflies, like other insects, have an exoskeleton. An exoskeleton is a hard outer coating that supports the insect's body. The exoskeleton is not like skin on a person, it does not grow as the insect grows. When an insect is too big for its exoskeleton, it sheds it or breaks out of it and grows a new one!

Monarch Butterfly

Looks
Monarch butterflies are bright orange and black. They are the most common butterflies in North America from May until November.

Lunch
Monarch butterflies eat mostly milkweed, but they also sip nectar from lilacs, goldenrod, thistle, and red clover. Milkweed is poisonous to most birds so they do not eat monarch butterflies.

Location
You do not have to travel far to find a monarch- in fact, you may have even seen one flying through your yard! Monarchs that are born in the spring and early summer usually live for just a few weeks. Monarchs that are born in midsummer migrate. Monarchs migrate to warmer places in the winter. Some monarchs are known to fly over 2,500 miles in just six weeks!

Range and Habitat
Butterflies are native to almost all parts of the world except Antarctica and the oceans. Butterflies are found in many different types of habitats including temperate habitats, mountain habitats, and tropical habitats.

Temperate Butterflies
A temperate region is where summers are warm and winters are cold. Butterflies that live in these regions must be able to either survive during the winter or migrate to a warmer climate. Temperate region butterflies are found in two types of habitats; grasslands and woodlands.

- Grasslands: Grassland butterflies can be found in the long grasses of meadows and flowery fields. Examples of grassland butterflies include the Adonis Blue, Common Crescentspot, and the Meadow Brown.
- Woodland: Woodland butterflies live near streams, among the treetops, or along the edges of woodland clearings. Examples of woodland butterflies include the Common Glider, Pine White, and the Acadian Hairstreak.

Mountain Butterflies
Mountain habitats can be very harsh and animals, including butterflies, must be able to survive the short summer, cold nights, and strong winds found in most treeless mountain habitats. Mountain butterflies are able to retain heat in their bodies through long, hairy scales. Some are dark colors which allow them to absorb the warmth of the sun quickly. Butterflies that live in mountain habitats include the Zephyr Blue, Piedmont Ringlet, and the Northern Marblewing.

Tropical Butterflies
Some of the most colorful butterflies in the world live in tropical habitats. Tropical rainforests do not have winter and stay warm and wet all year. A large variety of plants grow in tropical rainforests making them one of the most perfect homes for butterflies! Tropical butterflies include the Birdwing Swallowtail, Mother of Pearl, and the Yellow-bodied Clubtail.

> More than 6,000 species of butterflies live in Peru, a tropical nation located in South America.

Buckeye Butterfly

Looks
Buckeye butterflies look like they have big eyes on their wings called "eyespots." The eyespots do not really see, but they actually blink at birds trying to attack them. This scares the bird for a second and gives the buckeye time to fly away! In addition, to their eyespots, buckeyes have bright red bars on the front of their wings.

Lunch
Buckeyes sip water from puddles and nectar from milkweed, knapweed, asters, peppermint, and sunflowers.

Location
Buckeyes like to rest on the ground in the sun and can be found on the road, in a field, or in a meadow on a sunny, hot day. They can also be found chasing other butterflies and even grasshoppers!

Diet

The diet of a butterfly depends on what stage it is in its life cycle. In the larva stage, most caterpillars eat leaves (some will eat seeds, pods, or flowers at this stage). There are even a few types of **carnivorous** caterpillars that eat aphids and other caterpillars.

Adult butterflies eat by using their proboscis to suck nectar from plants. Some eat rotting fruit, tree sap, bird droppings, or animal dung. Many adult butterflies also drink liquid from wet sand or mud along streams or creeks.

Pollination

Pollination is the process where one plant receives **pollen** from another plant of the same type or species. Pollination must happen in order for new flowers to grow. Some plants are pollinated by the wind, but insects like butterflies, pollinate many plants.

Pollen is a sticky fluffy substance that forms inside flowers. Many types of pollen are yellow and you can look inside the middle of a flower and see it. Pollen looks a lot like a yellow dust.

When a butterfly stops at a flower to drink nectar, tiny grains of pollen stick to its body then, when it moves on to another flower, the pollen grains slip off. This pollinates the flowers.

Without pollination many types of flowers would become extinct.

Tiger Swallowtail Butterfly

Looks
The tiger swallowtail has bright yellow and black stripes like a tiger. They fly high in the air by the tallest tree branches between April and September. The wings of a swallowtail stretch to about six inches wide.

Lunch
Tiger swallowtails sip nectar from phlox, honeysuckle, and lilacs. They also drink water from puddles and streams. Swallowtails need the sodium from water in order to mate. They are actually able to sip the nectar while their wings are still beating! Talk about eating on the run!

Location
Swallowtails usually stay in groups and you may find them along the edges of a stream or even a puddle. The male swallowtail gives off a sweet smell that even you might be able to smell!

Life Cycle

"If nothing ever changed, there'd be no butterflies."
~Author Unknown

You may already know that butterflies start out as caterpillars, but how can that be? They do not look alike at all! Caterpillars and butterflies do have one major thing in common- change! The life cycle of the butterfly is an amazing process! Butterflies go through four special stages in their lives: egg, larva/caterpillar, pupa, and adult. The life cycle for a butterfly may only last a few weeks or it could last for several years! A butterfly spends most of its life hidden on a leaf or the underside of a branch and only going out into the world when it reaches the adult stage.

1. Egg Stage

This stage begins when a female butterfly lays her eggs on a plant that can be used for food by her babies when they hatch. Butterflies lay an average of only 100 eggs in their entire lifetime. Of those 100 eggs, only about two will survive!

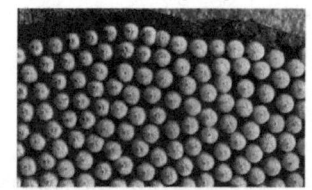

Butterfly eggs come in a variety of sizes, shapes, and colors. They can be found on the bottoms of leaves and on stems. Once in a while they are found on old logs and stumps. Some types of butterfly eggs hatch in just a few days or weeks and others take as long as several months to hatch.

Sitting on a plant unprotected makes a butterfly egg an easy target for birds, frogs, mice, and carnivorous insects like ants and wasps. These creatures all love to eat butterfly eggs and are considered major predators of the butterfly.

Caterpillars

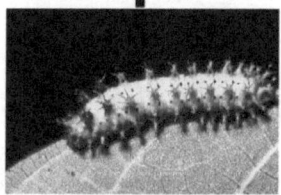

Caterpillars look a lot like worms, but they are not worms. They are actually butterflies in the larva stage of their life. A caterpillar's mouth is different from a butterfly's mouth because it is made for chewing leaves instead of sipping nectar. A caterpillar's body has six front legs that will be the butterfly's legs and then it has up to ten other legs, called prolegs. A caterpillar's prolegs disappear once it has molted for the last time.

All caterpillars make **silk**. If you own a silk scarf, tie, or ribbon- it was made of silk made by caterpillars!

2. Larva/Caterpillar Stage

Larva of a butterfly

When the egg finally hatches a little creature crawls out. This creature is called a larva, but you probably know it as a caterpillar. Just like butterflies and their eggs, caterpillars come in different sizes and colors. Some are smooth and shiny, some are hairy, and some are even covered with spines. The larva has six real legs and a bunch of prolegs. The six real legs have joints so they are bendable. They also have a little claw on each foot. The prolegs do not have joints and they have little hooks to help the caterpillar cling to things.

Once the larva is out of the egg, it only has one thing on its mind. Food! The newly hatched baby begins to eat the leaves of the plant on which it hatched. It keeps eating! And eating!! And eating!!! All of this eating makes the caterpillar grow very quickly. It grows so fast that it becomes too large for its skin. Because of this, it will need to shed its skin four to five times during this stage.

The caterpillar must be on the lookout for danger at all times. Many other animals like to make a nice meal out of a juicy looking caterpillar. Some of the predators that caterpillars have to beware of include rodents like mice and rats; reptiles like lizards; bats, spiders, birds, and insects.

> "Anyone who believes in Christ is a new creation. The old is gone! The new has come!"
>
> ~2 Corinthians 5:17

3. Pupa Stage

This is the important stage when a caterpillar changes into an adult butterfly. Once the larva has reached its full size, it spins a small thread of silk on a leaf or twig to which it attaches itself. At this point some caterpillars will spin a silk **cocoon** around themselves, but most species do not. Finally, the last skin becomes a hardened case called the **pupa** or **chrysalis.**

4. Adult Stage

Stage 4 is the most awesome and exciting stage of a butterfly's life cycle. Inside the pupa, something happens that even scientists cannot explain. The creature that was once a caterpillar becomes almost a liquid. It then reforms into a completely new shape! The extreme changes in a butterfly's looks and habits are called **metamorphosis**. Metamorphosis means sudden change. Once its new shape is complete it pushes itself out of the chrysalis. This is the final adult stage. It is now a butterfly!

Predators and Defense
Predators
Butterflies have many predators to watch out for including:
- Birds
- Bats
- Lizards
- Spiders
- Other insects

Defense Mechanisms
A defense mechanism is a special instinct that helps an animal protect itself from predators. Butterflies and caterpillars have several types of defense mechanisms including:

- Camouflage: One type of defense mechanism that butterflies and caterpillars use is **camouflage**. During the different stages of its life cycle a butterfly has certain colors or characteristics that help it blend into its environment. Camouflage makes the butterfly look like a rock or leaf or even part of a tree or plant. Camouflage allows them to blend in so well that it is nearly impossible to see them. This mechanism is what helps the butterfly avoid being eaten.
- Poison: Another defense mechanism is poison. Some butterflies and caterpillars are actually poisonous to other animals that may eat them. When a predator eats a poisonous butterfly it becomes very sick. The predator learns not to eat any butterflies like the one that made it sick! A lot of non-poisonous butterflies have markings or patterns on their wings that are similar to poisonous ones. When predators see the markings, they avoid eating any butterfly that looks like the poisonous one. This defense, called **mimicry**, helps keep non-poisonous butterflies safe from predators too!
- Flight: The best defense a butterfly has is its ability to fly. Different species of butterflies can fly at different speeds. The speeds vary from five miles per hour to as fast as 30 miles per hour. Most poisonous types of butterflies are slower than the non-poisonous types.

Hibernation and Migration

"Just living is not enough," said the butterfly, "one must have sunshine, freedom and a little flower."
~Hans Christian Anderson

Butterflies are cold-blooded animals. This means that their body temperature goes down when the temperature outside goes down. They need a warm body temperature in order to fly, so when the sun goes down or the climate changes to cold, butterflies cannot fly. Butterflies rely on a warm climate to keep their bodies warm and to produce vegetation and flowers for them eat. In areas that have cold winter climates, the vegetation becomes dormant or dies in the winter and butterflies must either migrate to a warmer climate or hibernate in order to survive.

Hibernation

When you think of an animal hibernating, you might think of a bear sleeping away the winter in its cozy den. But other animals hibernate too, including butterflies! Some butterflies survive the winter as eggs, caterpillars, or pupae; and others survive as adult butterflies by hibernating. When a butterfly hibernates, it goes into a state of inactivity. Its body functions slow down so much that the butterfly does not even need to eat. Butterflies hibernate in caves, hollow trees, under leaves, in sheds, or even inside houses. Butterflies that are hibernating are harmless and should be left alone for the winter.

Migration

Most butterflies migrate when changes in the environment like cold winter weather, take place. Migration is when an animal leaves one area and moves to another that is miles away. Most butterflies only migrate short distances, but a few species migrate thousands of miles each year. In addition, some butterflies do not live long enough to make a round-trip in migration. They do stop and lay eggs along the way so that new butterflies join the group for the rest of their trip!

For example, the monarch is a butterfly commonly found in the United States. Monarchs that live east of the Rocky Mountains often migrate to tree clusters on the coast of California. Monarchs that live to the west of the Rocky Mountains migrate to the warm areas just north of Mexico and into Mexico.

Did You Know?

In Europe, the Small Tortoiseshell and the Peacock butterflies both hibernate during the winter. These two types of butterflies are often seen hibernating in backyard sheds and even houses!

A monarch butterfly flag is flown each fall as soon as migrating monarchs arrive in Santa Cruz, California. The flag is flown for six months, until the last monarch flies for the north.

Is It A **Butterfly** Or A **Moth**?

Butterflies and moths belong to a large group, called an **order**, of animals. This order is called the Lepidopteron and comes from the Greek words for "scale" and "wing." There are about 160,000 known species of butterflies and moths in the order. It is often difficult to tell the difference between butterflies and moths, but there are some very definite ones. Differences between the two include:

- Time of Day: Most butterflies fly during the day and most moths fly at night.
- Wing Position: When a butterfly is resting, it holds its wings up and together. Moths keep their wings down and flat when resting.
- Color: Most butterflies are beautiful colors. Most moths are usually dull colors.
- Antennae Ball: Butterfly antennae have little round balls at the ends. Most moths do not. Some moths even have antennae that look fuzzy or like feathers!

Butterfly Collecting and Gardening

Butterfly collecting is a popular hobby for many. It is O.K. to catch most types of butterflies, but collectors need to be aware of what types are protected by law. In addition, many parks and reserves have special guidelines to follow when capturing wildlife. If a collector is unsure if a certain butterfly is endangered, he or she should just draw a picture or take a photo of it. Most serious collectors write down where they captured their butterflies and this helps scientists understand their habitats and helps them with conservation.

Extinct Butterflies of the World

Xerces Blue butterfly (United States)

Large Copper butterfly (Europe)

Black-veined White butterfly (Britain)

Endangered Butterflies of the World

Philippine Swallowtail (Philippines)

Regal Fritillary butterfly (Canada and parts of United States)

Corsican Swallowtail (Corsica and Sardinia)

Queen Alexandra's Birdwing (New Guinea)

Black-veined White butterfly (Europe)

Zebra Swallowtail (Canada and parts of United States)

An alternative method to collecting butterflies in the wild is to raise them yourself! Caterpillars can be raised in netted enclosures that have plenty of food and fresh air. This enables a collector to watch the stages that a caterpillar goes through to become a butterfly.

Another alternative to collecting is butterfly watching. This includes photographing butterflies, sketching butterflies, and butterfly gardening. Butterfly watching is a lot like bird watching. The watcher tracks and observes butterflies using binoculars or a camera and recording what he or she sees. Some watchers use a net to catch a butterfly to observe it more closely and then release it back into the wild.

Butterfly gardens are great ways to attract butterflies to your yard. If you want to attract butterflies, simply plant nectar flowers that butterflies like to sip. First, you need to find out what kinds of butterflies are found in your region. You can find this out in a field guide for butterflies. Next, choose a spot for your garden and decide what flowers you will plant. Your local greenhouse or nursery can help you pick plants that are suitable for a butterfly garden. Remember not to use insecticides on your garden! Some nectar flowers that attract butterflies include:

- Butterfly bush
- Clover
- Dogbane
- Hollyhock
- Lantana
- Sassafras
- Thistle
- Verbena
- Willow
- Zinnia

Conservation

Over the past 50 years, five different butterfly species have become extinct. There are now 55 species living on Earth and their populations have decreased. Natural butterfly habitats and food sources have been destroyed by the growth of the modern world. Because of this, butterfly conservation groups have formed all over the world to guard the remaining species. Conservation means to protect, keep safe, and to restore.

These groups remind people, especially gardeners, to be kind to butterflies. They also ask gardeners to grow flowers that are butterfly friendly. They develop special places for butterflies where they will be safe and can increase in population. They raise butterflies and then return them to their natural environments. They also help to restore lost habitats.

Butterflies play an important role in the earth's environment. Without them we would lose some other beautiful parts of nature like many types of flowers. If you catch a butterfly to examine it, remember to be very gentle and release it back into its natural habitat when you are done!

Coffee Filter Butterflies
Materials
- Coffee filter
- Markers
- Wooden clothes pins
- Pipe cleaners
- Spray bottle of water

Instructions
- Color each coffee filter with many colors using markers
- Spray the entire coffee filter with water to give it a tied dyed look
- Let dry
- Pinch coffee filter together in the middle and attach clothes pin to center
- Attach pipe cleaners to the top for antennae

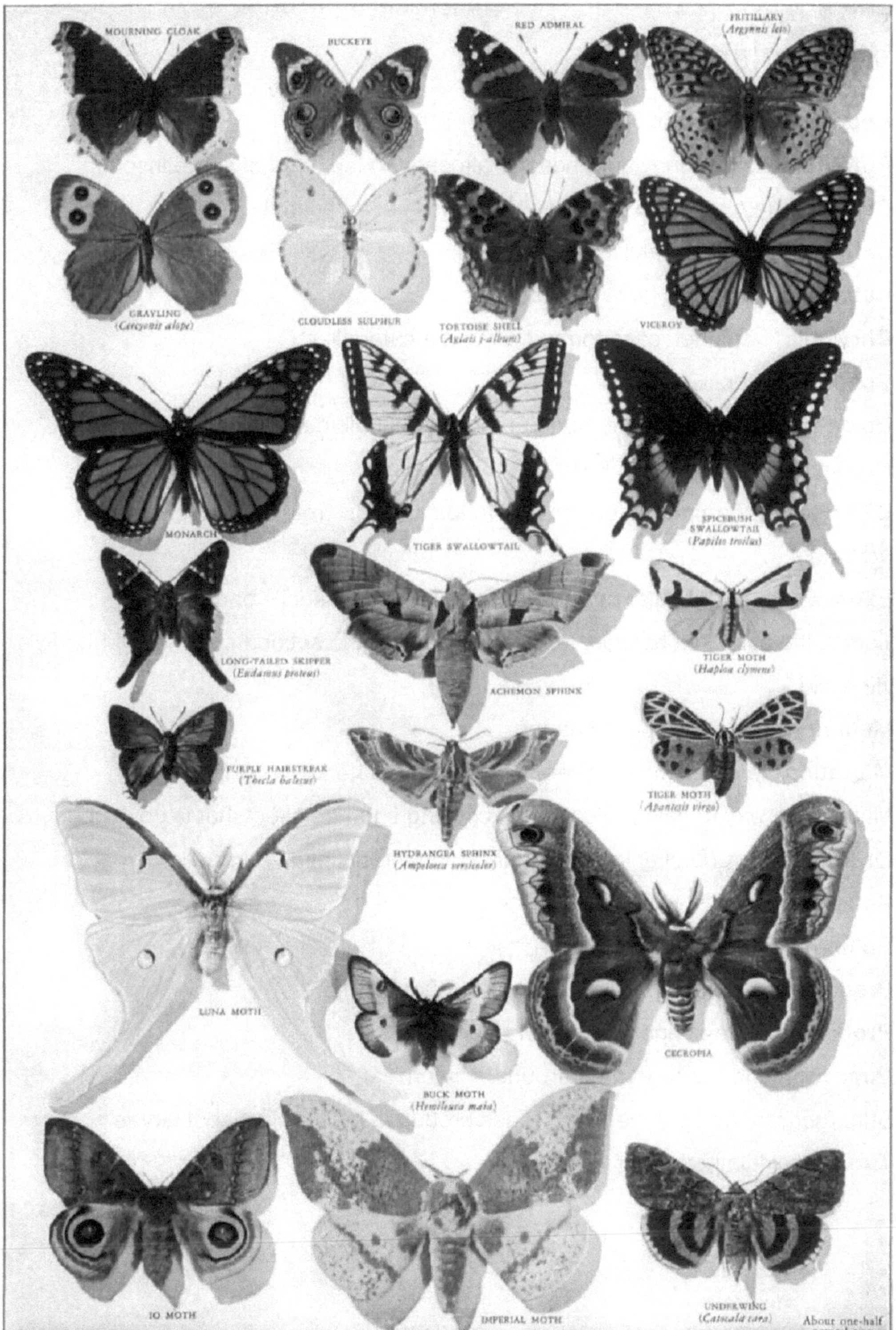

About one-half natural size

Vocabulary

Abdomen: end part of an insect

Antennae: long, skinny appendages attached to the head of some insects

Camouflage: protective coloring that helps hide an animal

Carnivorous: meat eater

Caterpillar: wormlike larva of a butterfly

Chrysalis: hardened case formed around a caterpillar

Cocoon: protective case

Compound eye: large eye made up of many smaller eyes that see in units

Conservation: to protect, keep safe, and restore

Defense mechanism: a feature that helps animals protect themselves from predators

Exoskeleton: hard outer coating that supports the insect's body

Larva: the baby that hatches from an egg during the second stage of a butterfly's life cycle

Metamorphosis: complete change

Migration: when animals leave one area for another area

Mimicry: a way to gain protection by copying another insect that is poisonous

Order: large group of animals organized for classification purposes

Pollen: yellow dust made by flowers

Pollination: the transfer of pollen

Predator: an animal that lives by eating other animals

Proboscis: tube-shaped tongue of a butterfly

Pupa: hardened case formed around a caterpillar

Silk: fabric made from the fine threads produced by certain insect larvae

Thorax: middle part of an insect

Activity 1

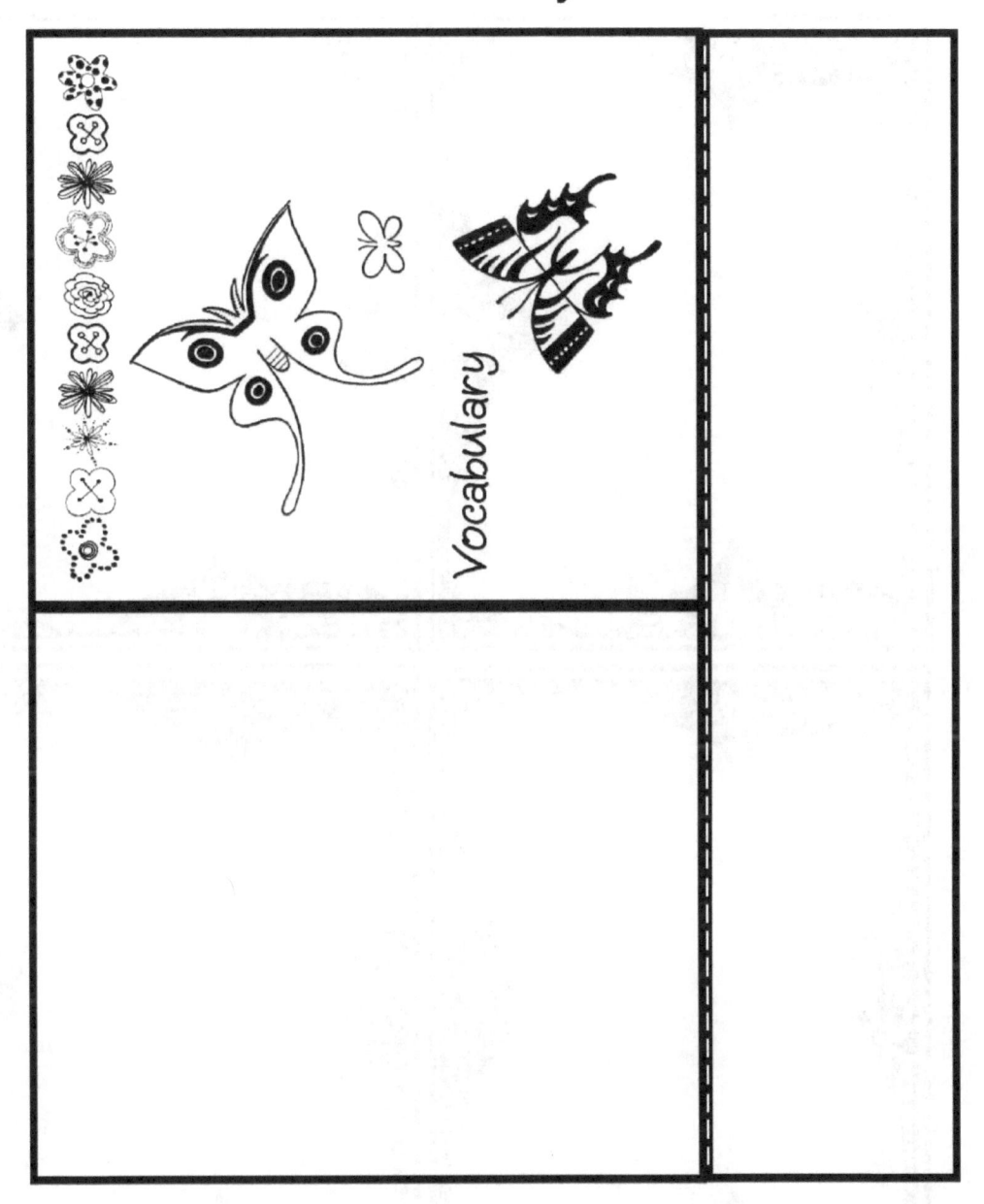

Vocabulary

Activity 1

Activity 1

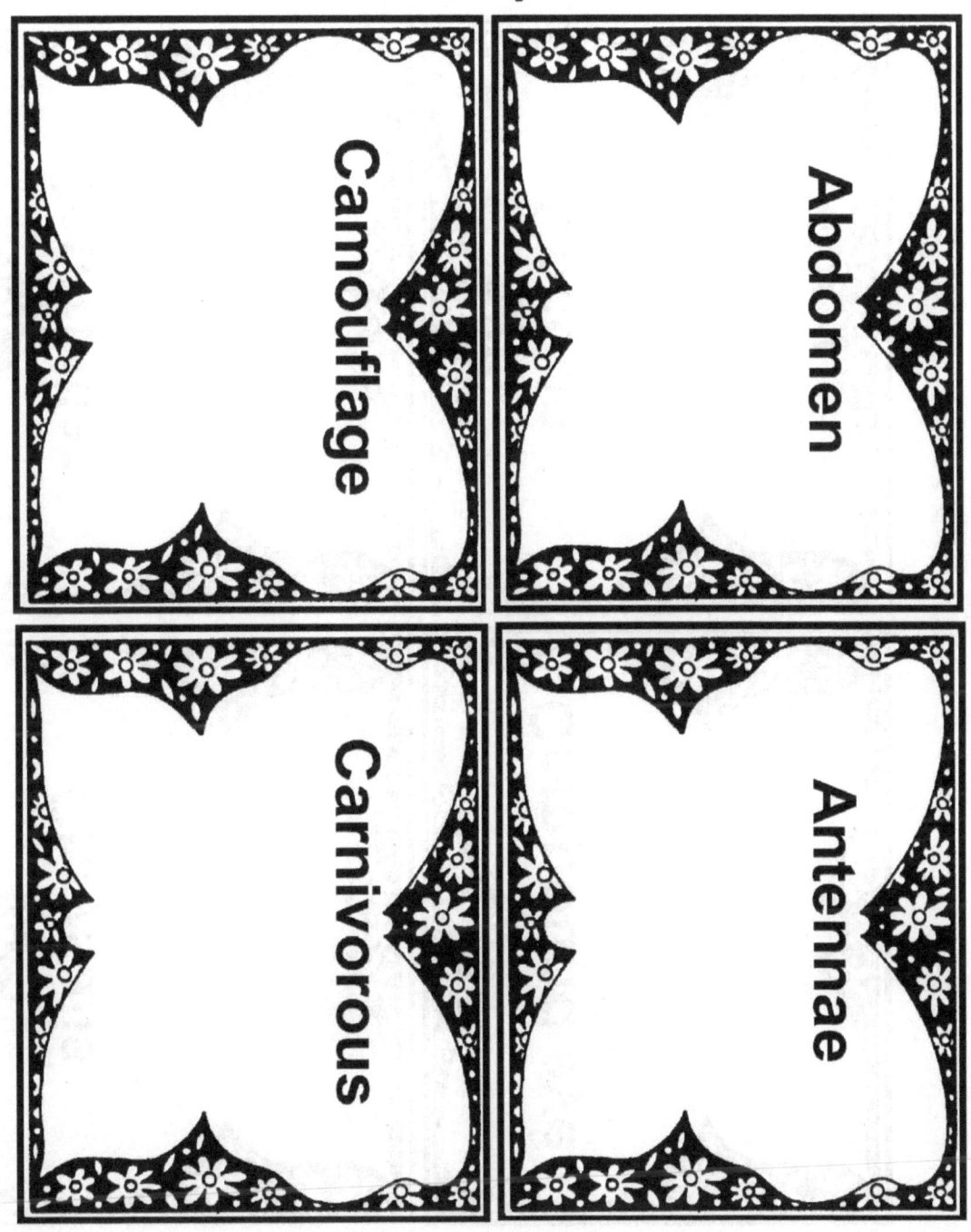

Camouflage	Abdomen
Carnivorous	Antennae

Activity 1

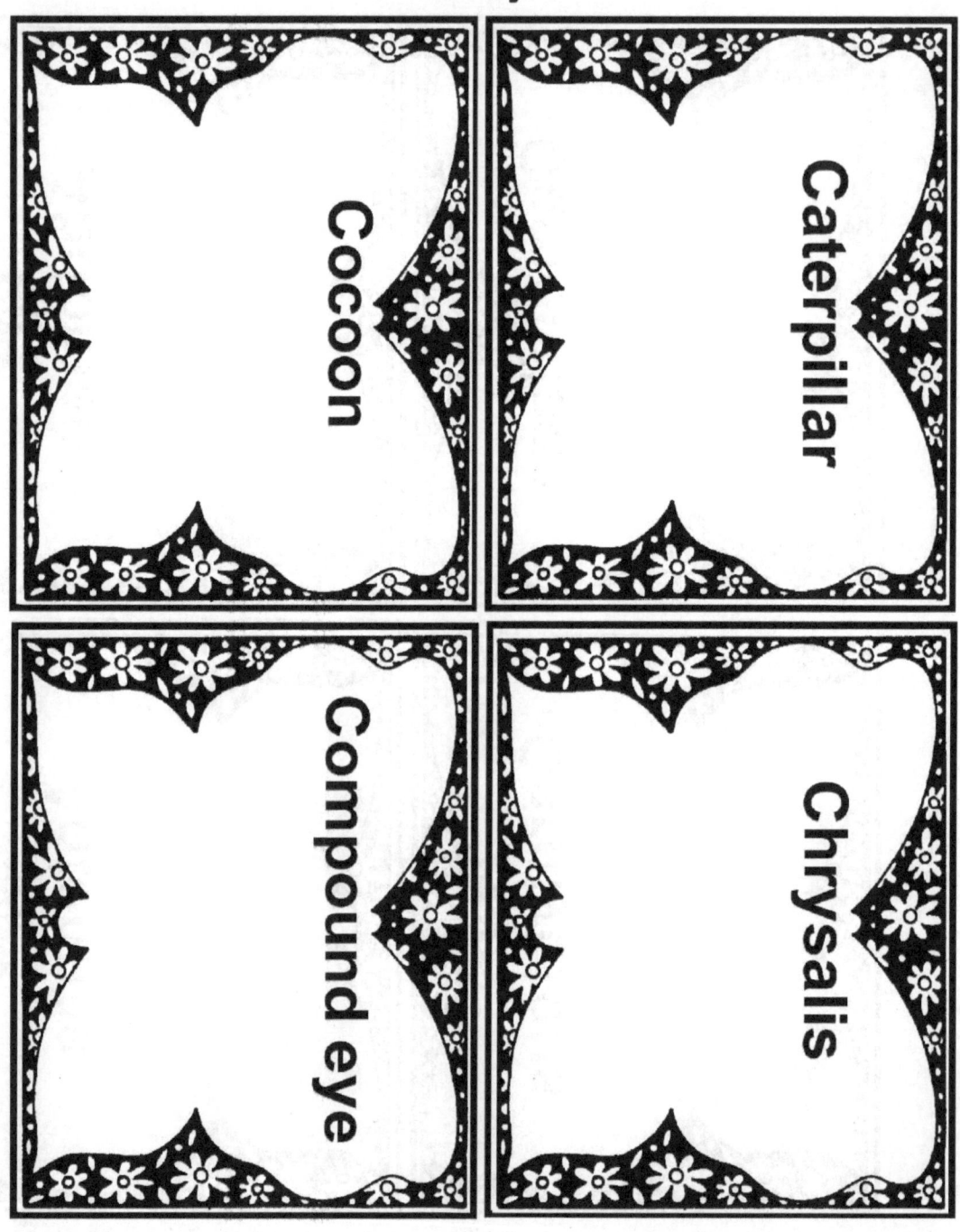

Cocoon	Caterpillar
Compound eye	Chrysalis

Activity 1

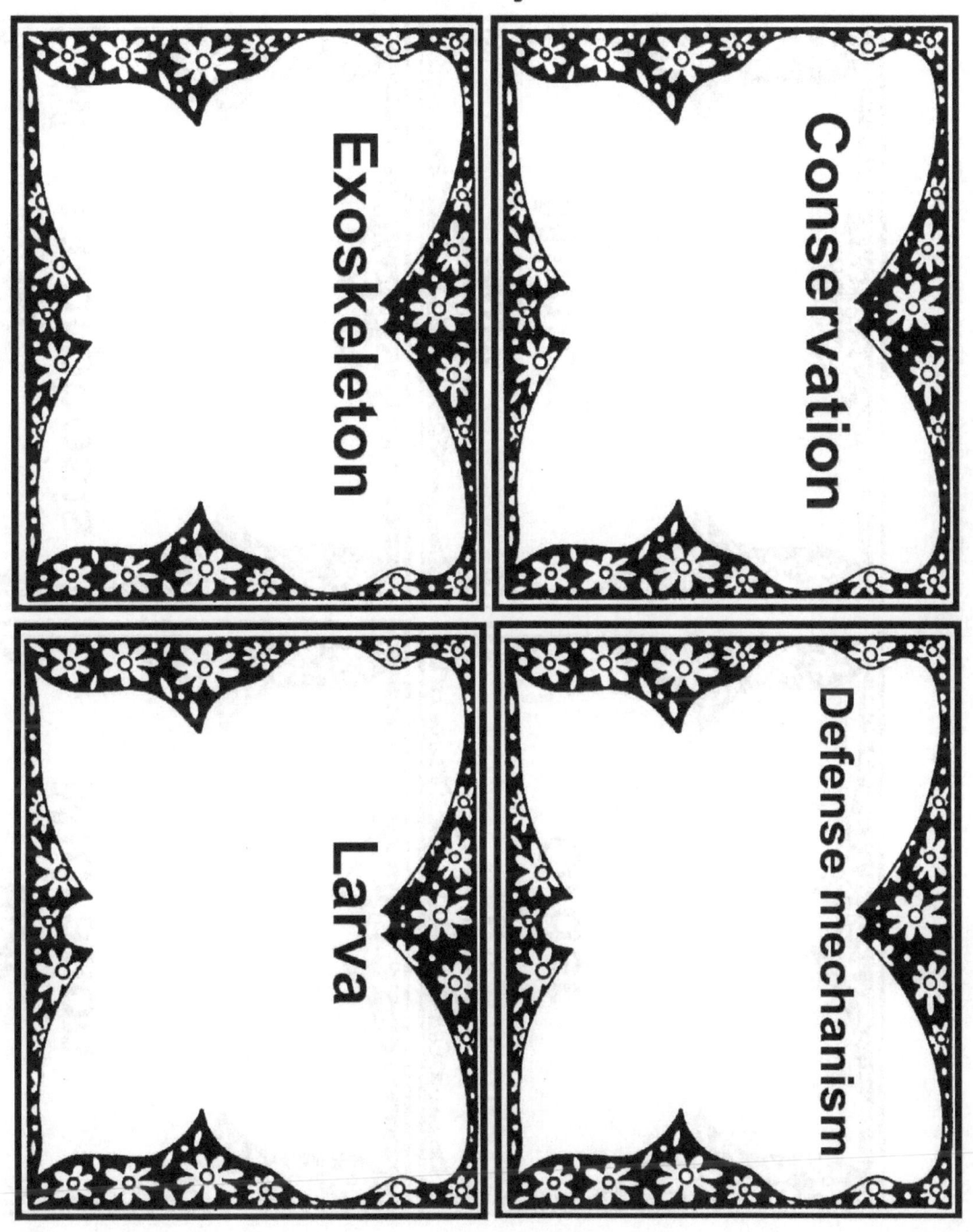

Conservation	**Exoskeleton**
Defense mechanism	**Larva**

Activity 1

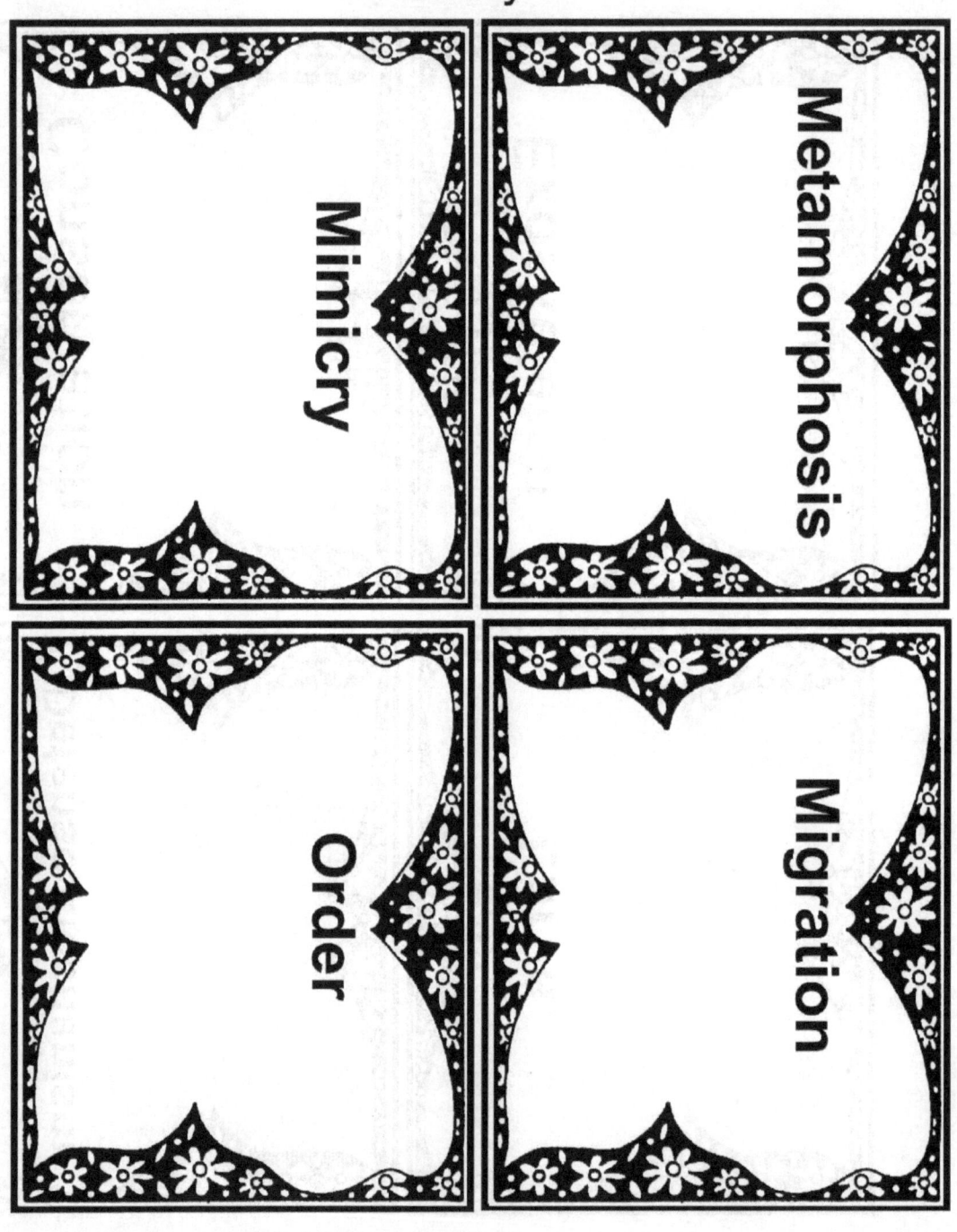

Mimicry	Metamorphosis
Order	Migration

Activity 1

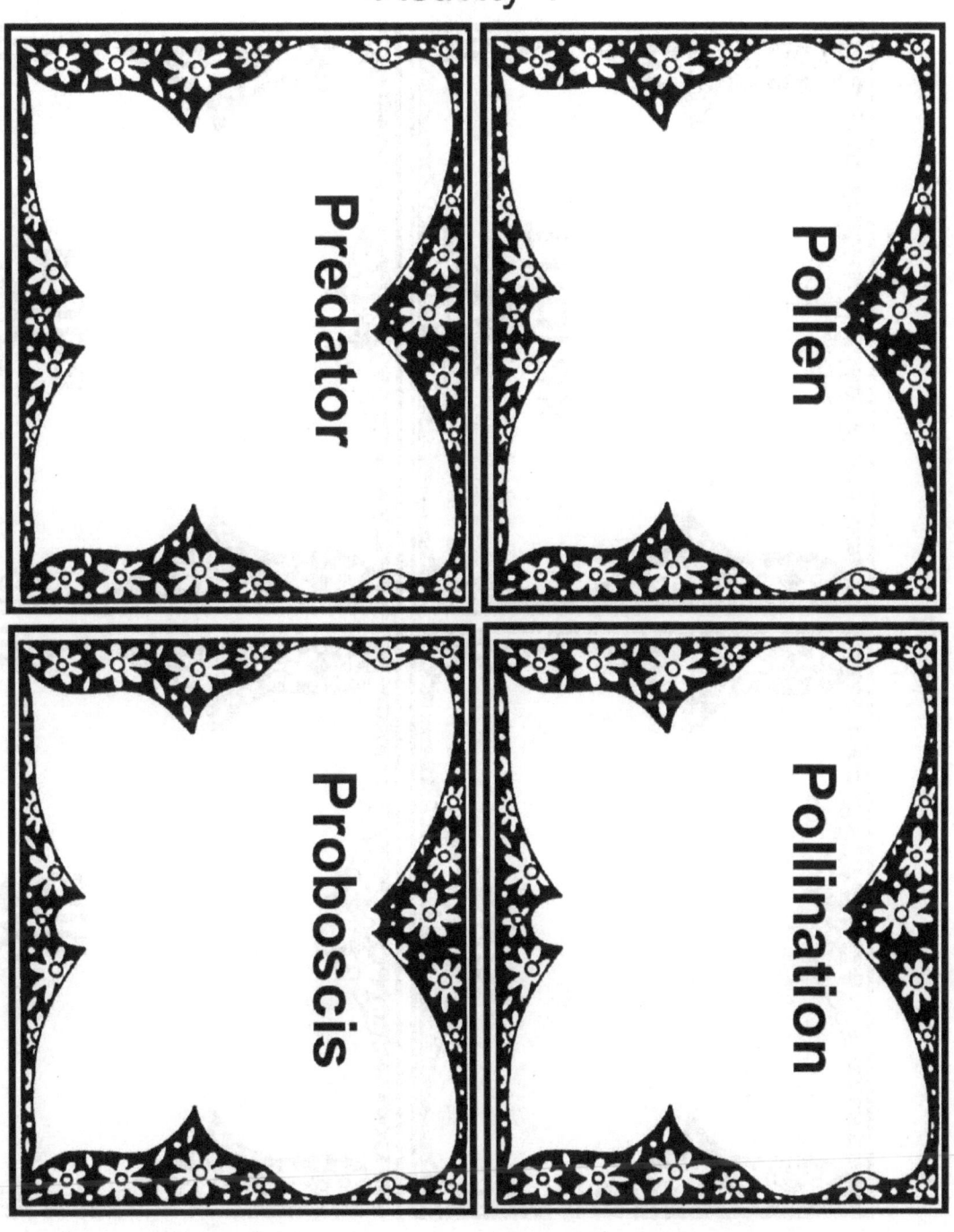

Predator	Pollen
Proboscis	Pollination

Activity 1

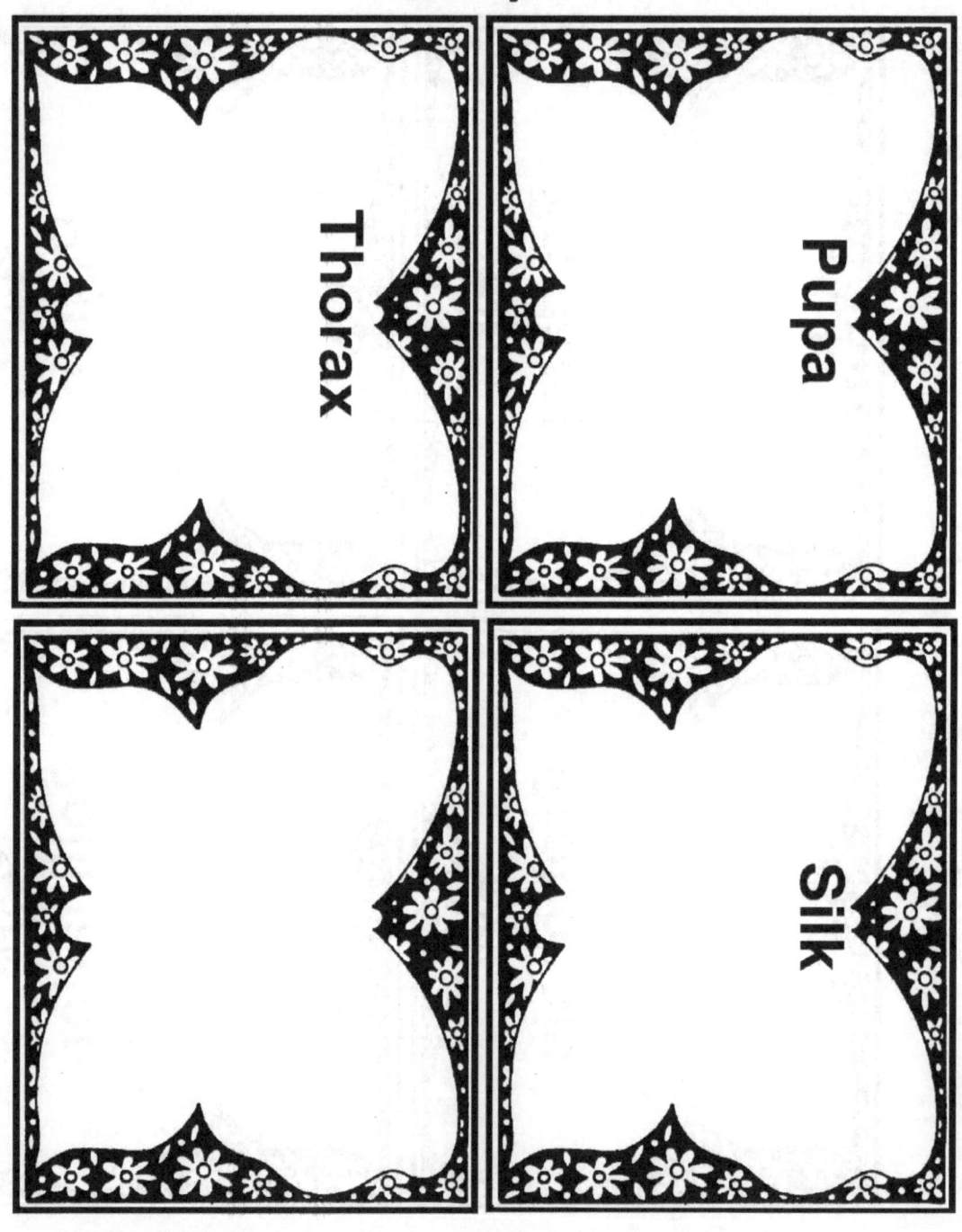

Thorax	Pupa
	Silk

40 | Page

Activity 1

- end part of an insect
- to protect, keep safe, and restore
- a way to gain protection by copying another insect that is poisonous
- long, skinny appendages attached to the head of some insects
- a feature that helps animals protect themselves from predators
- protective coloring that helps hide an animal meat eater
- hard outer coating that supports the insect's body
- large group of animals organized for classification purposes
- wormlike larva of a butterfly
- the baby that hatches from an egg during the second stage of a butterfly's life cycle
- hardened case formed around a caterpillar; protective case
- complete change
- yellow dust made by flowers
- large eye made up of many smaller eyes that see in units
- when animals leave one area for another area

Activity 1

- the transfer of pollen

- an animal that lives by eating other animals

- tube-shaped tongue of a butterfly

- hardened case formed around a caterpillar

- fabric made from the fine threads produced by certain insect larvae

- middle part of an insect

Activity 2

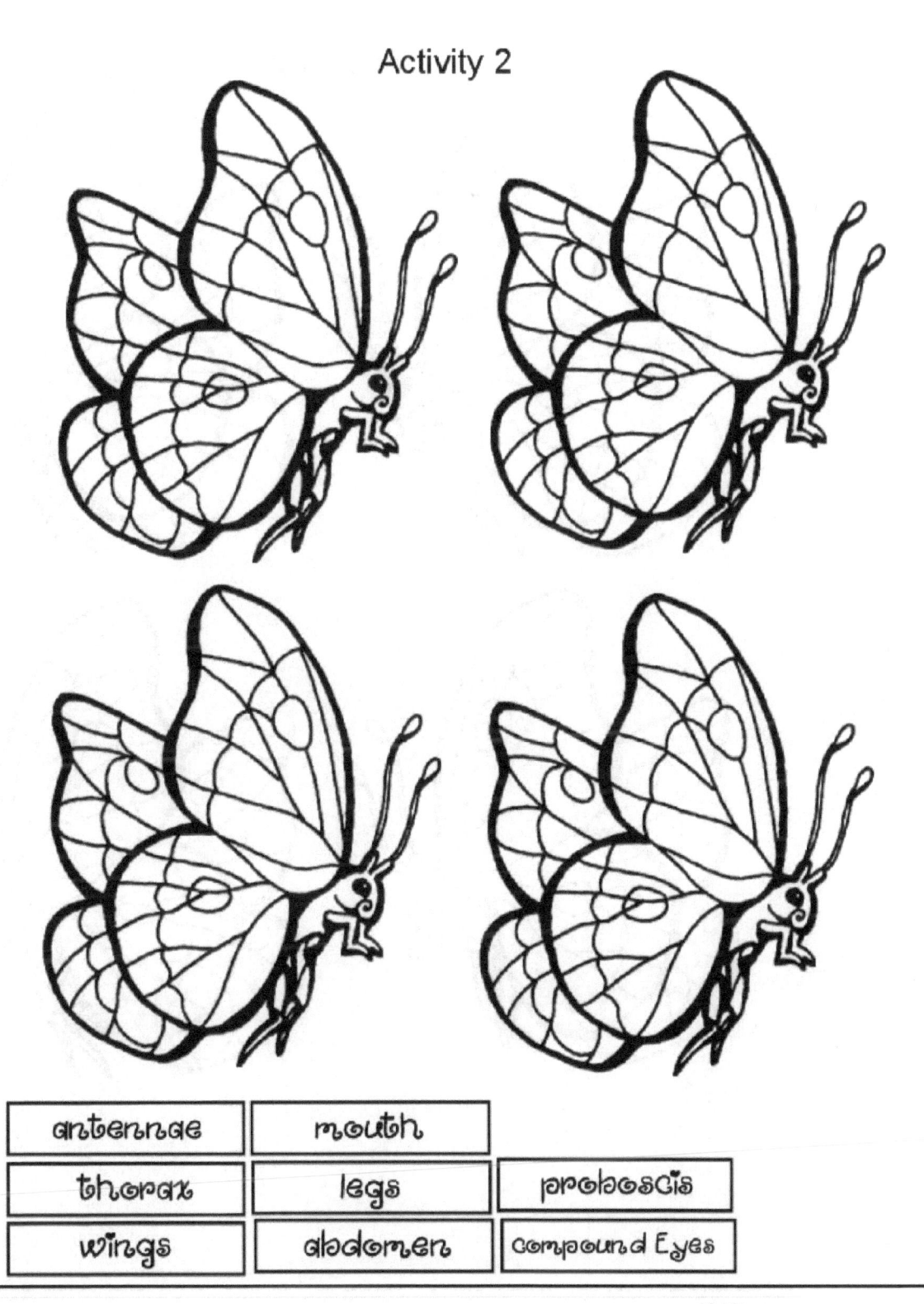

antennae	mouth	
thorax	legs	proboscis
wings	abdomen	compound Eyes

Activity 2

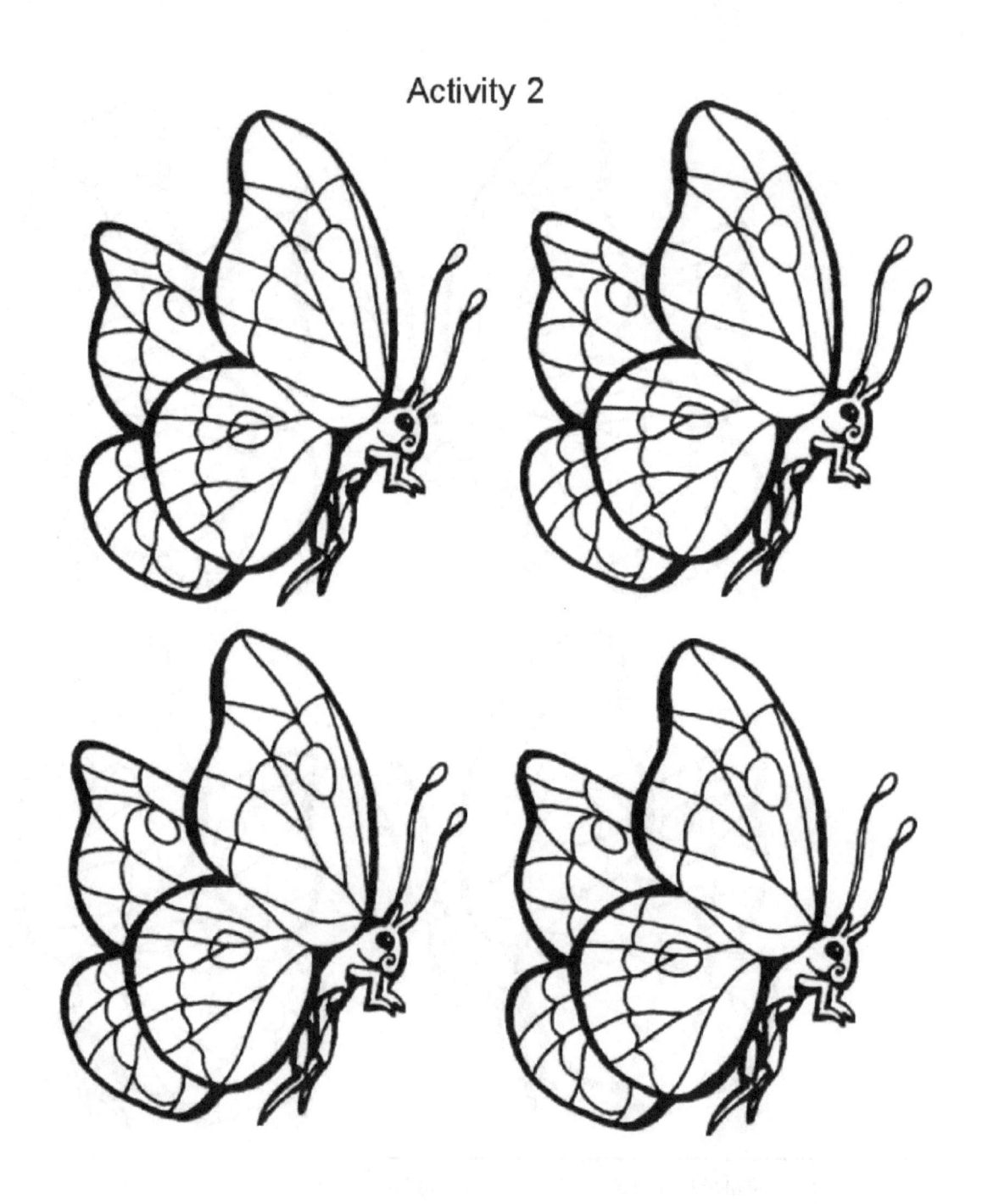

Activity 2

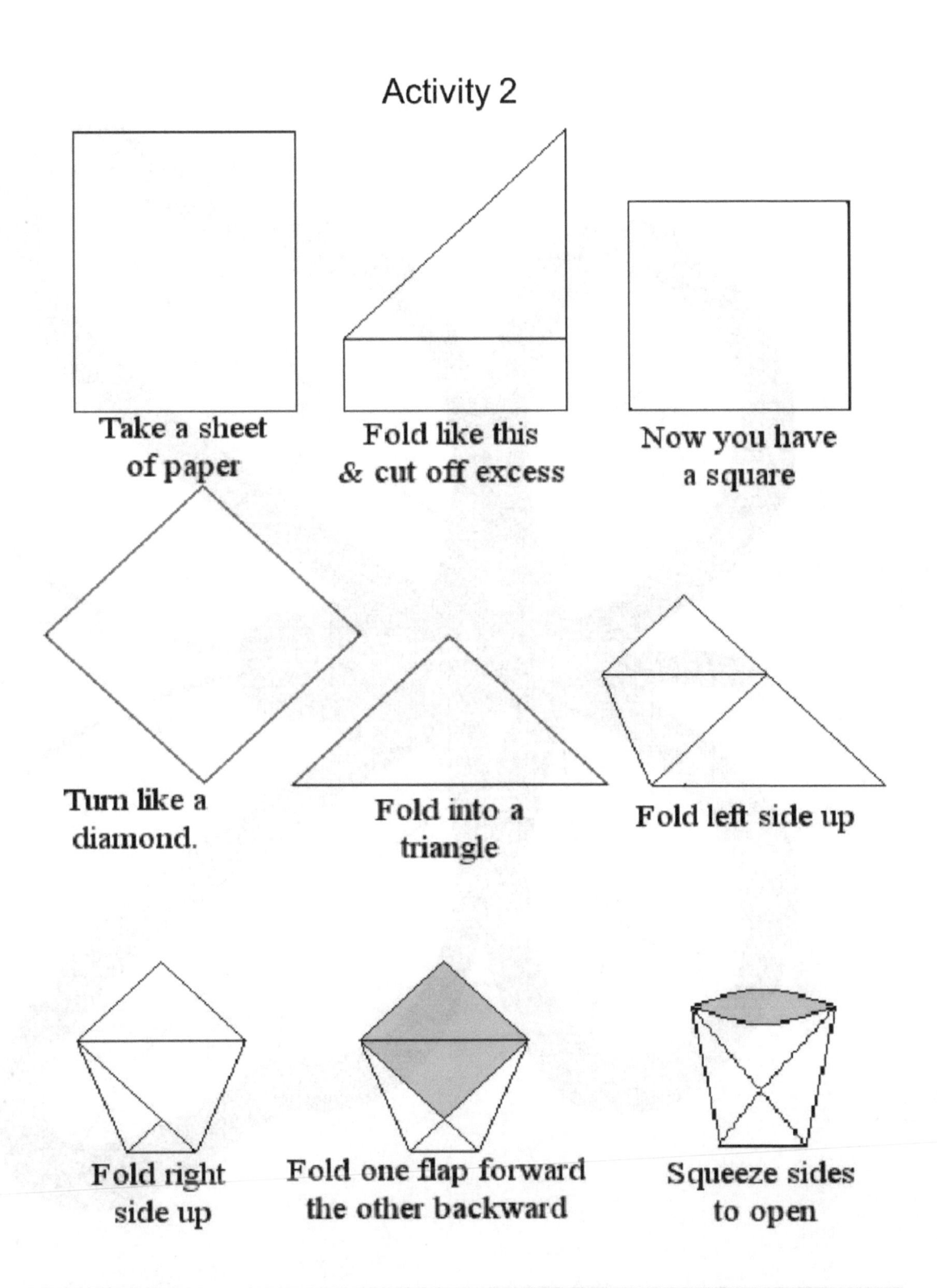

Take a sheet of paper	Fold like this & cut off excess	Now you have a square
Turn like a diamond.	Fold into a triangle	Fold left side up
Fold right side up	Fold one flap forward the other backward	Squeeze sides to open

Activity 3

Activity 3

Activity 4

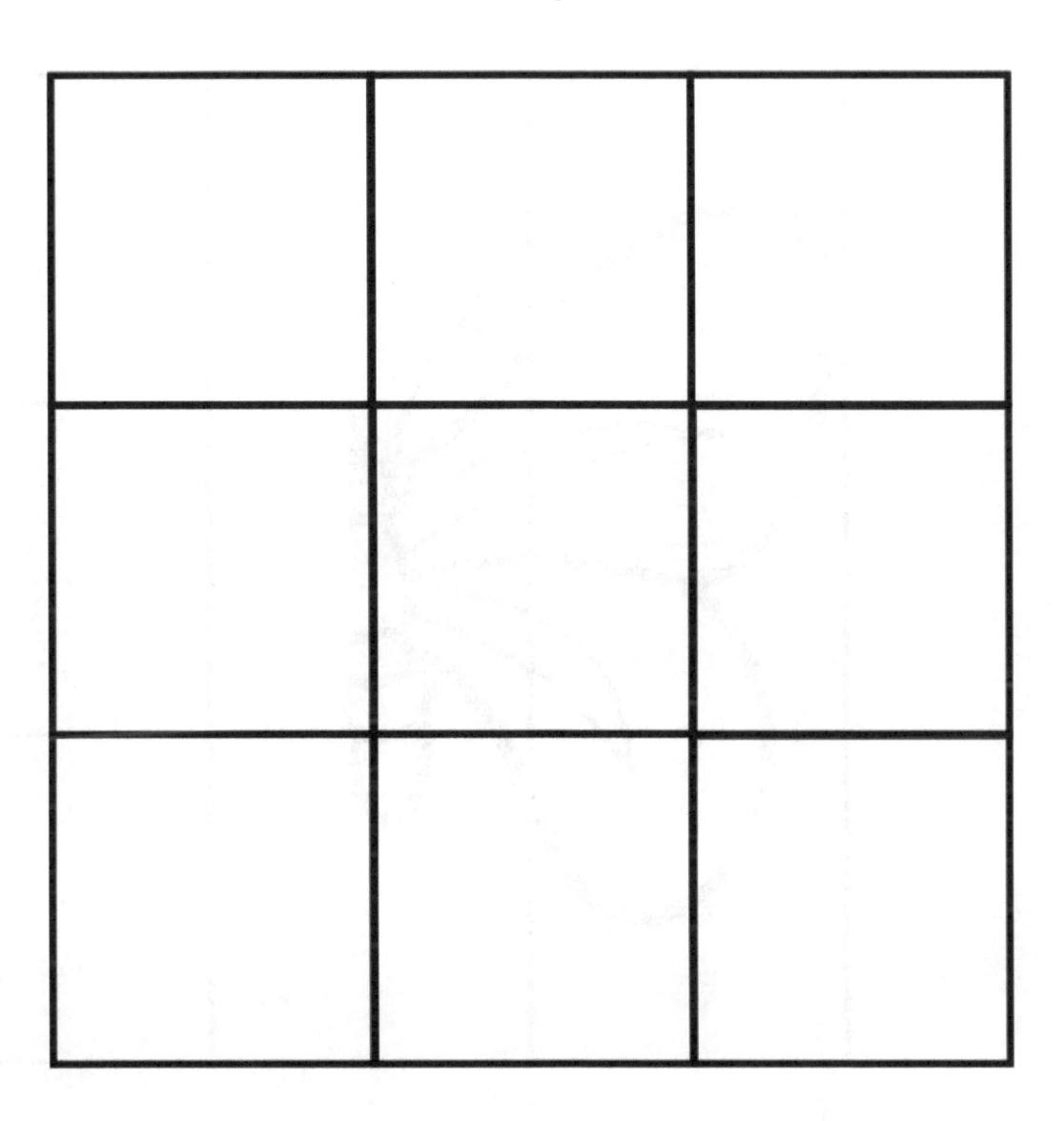

Activity 4

Activity 4

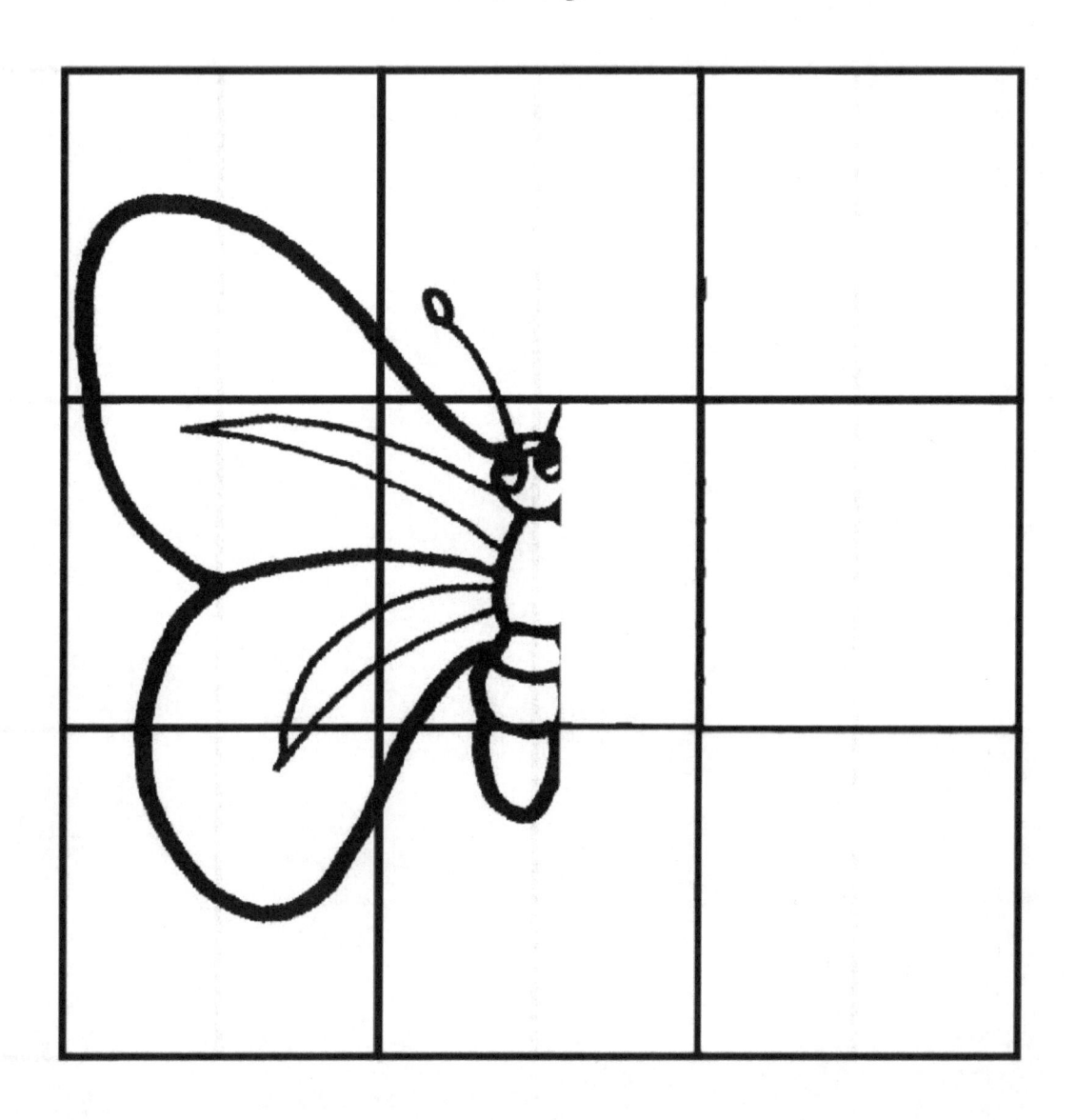

Activity 5

BUTTERFLY

LCMVNBOPQ

QIPPFUEMVQ

QOEICNDJFYG

CMVKFJDITEA

ALFIDEUFVIS

Activity 5

How Well Do Your Eyes See?	___ Feet Away Line 1_____ Line 2 _____ Line 3 _____ Line 4 _____ Line 5 _____ Line 6 _____
___ Feet Away Line 1_____ Line 2 _____ Line 3 _____ Line 4 _____ Line 5 _____ Line 6 _____	___ Feet Away Line 1_____ Line 2 _____ Line 3 _____ Line 4 _____ Line 5 _____ Line 6 _____

Activity 6

What
is an

Exoskeleton

Activity 7

HABITATS

Activity 7

A temperate region is where summers are warm and winters are cold.

A Mountain habitat has short summers, cold nights, and strong winds.

Tropical rainforests do not have winter and stay warm and wet all year.

Temperate

Mountain

Tropical

Activity 8

Activity 8

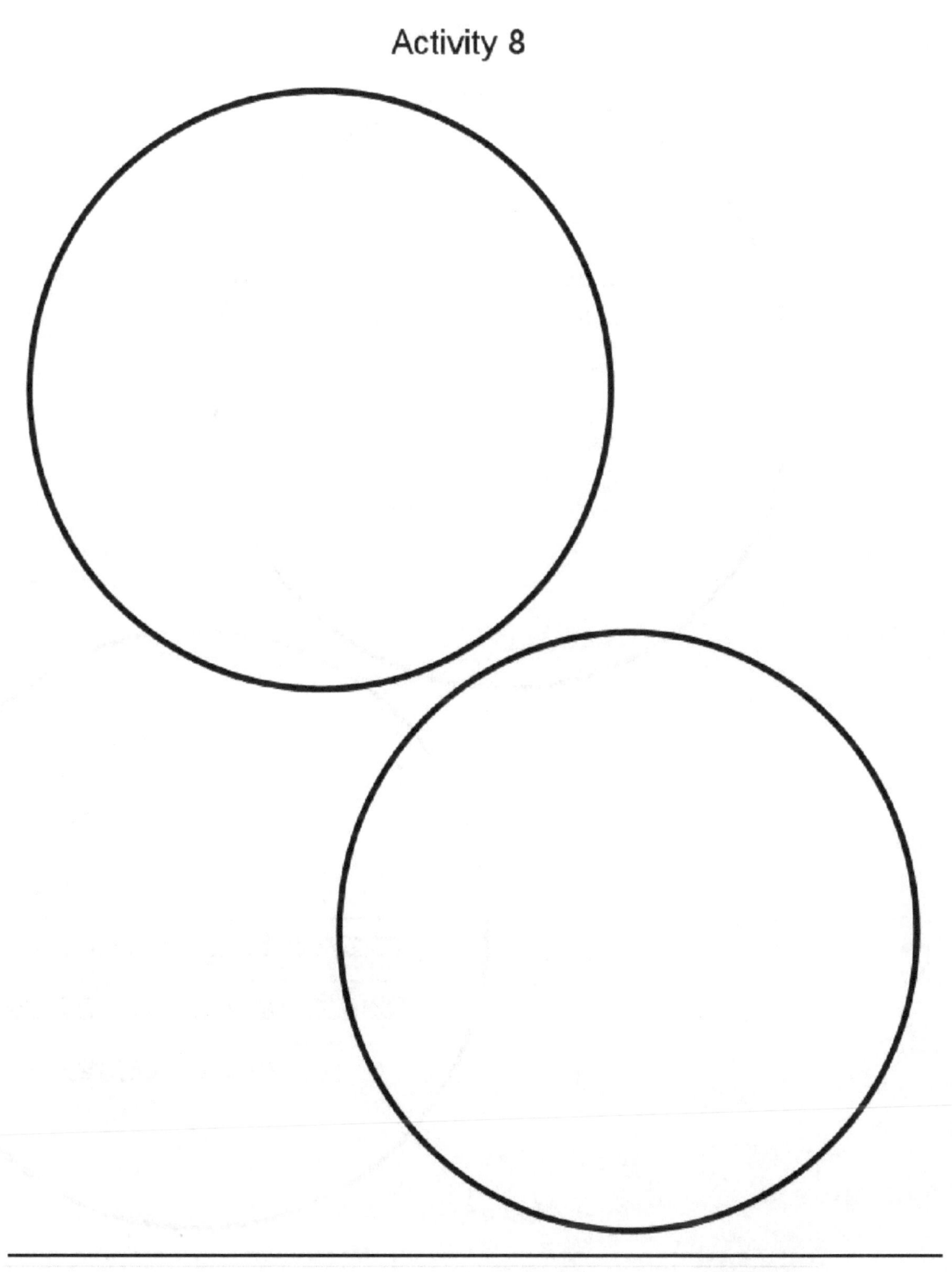

Activity 8

The diet of a butterfly depends on what stage it is in its life cycle.

In the larva stage, most caterpillars eat leaves (some will eat seeds, pods, or flowers at this stage).

Activity 8

There are even a few types of carnivorous caterpillars that eat aphids and other caterpillars.

Adult butterflies eat by using their proboscis to suck nectar from plants.

Activity 8

Some eat rotting fruit, tree sap, bird droppings, or animal dung.

Many adult butterflies also drink liquid from wet sand or mud along streams or creeks.

Activity 10

Pollination Sequence

Without pollination, many types of flowers would become extinct.

Activity 10

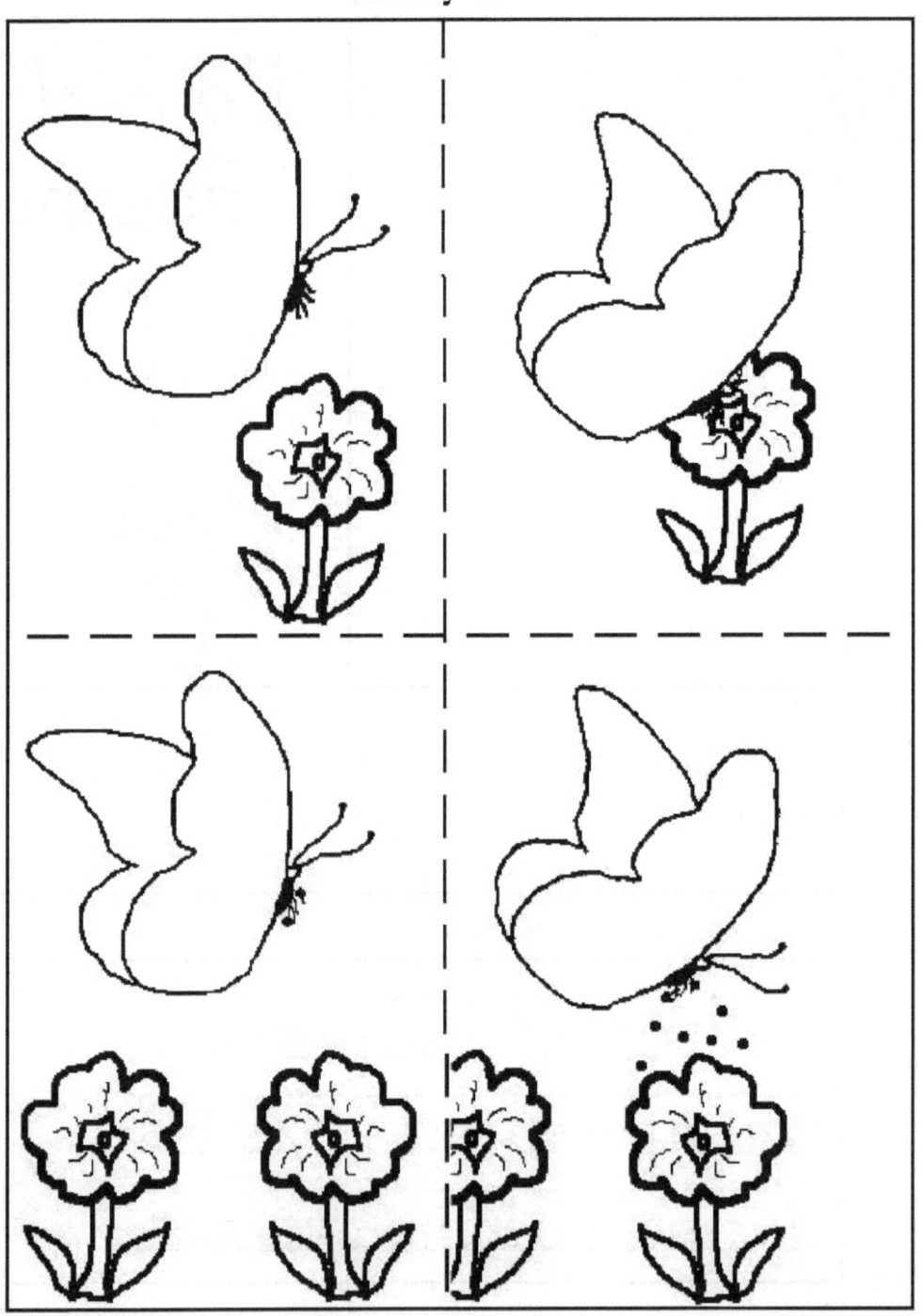

Activity 11

Life Cycle

Activity 12

Paste into matchbook and color 1 square for each egg that will survive.

How Many Eggs Will Survive?

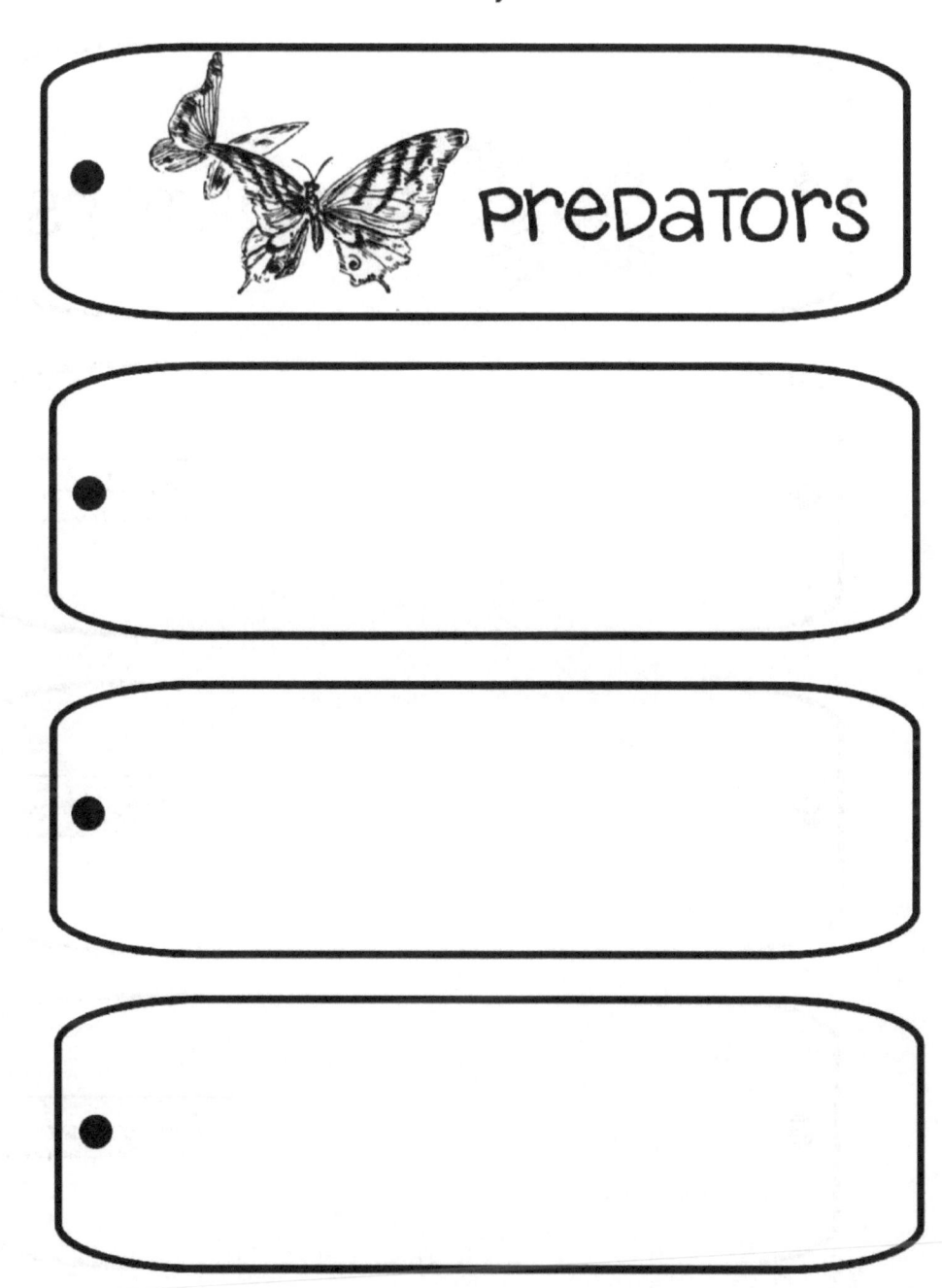

Activity 15

PREDATORS

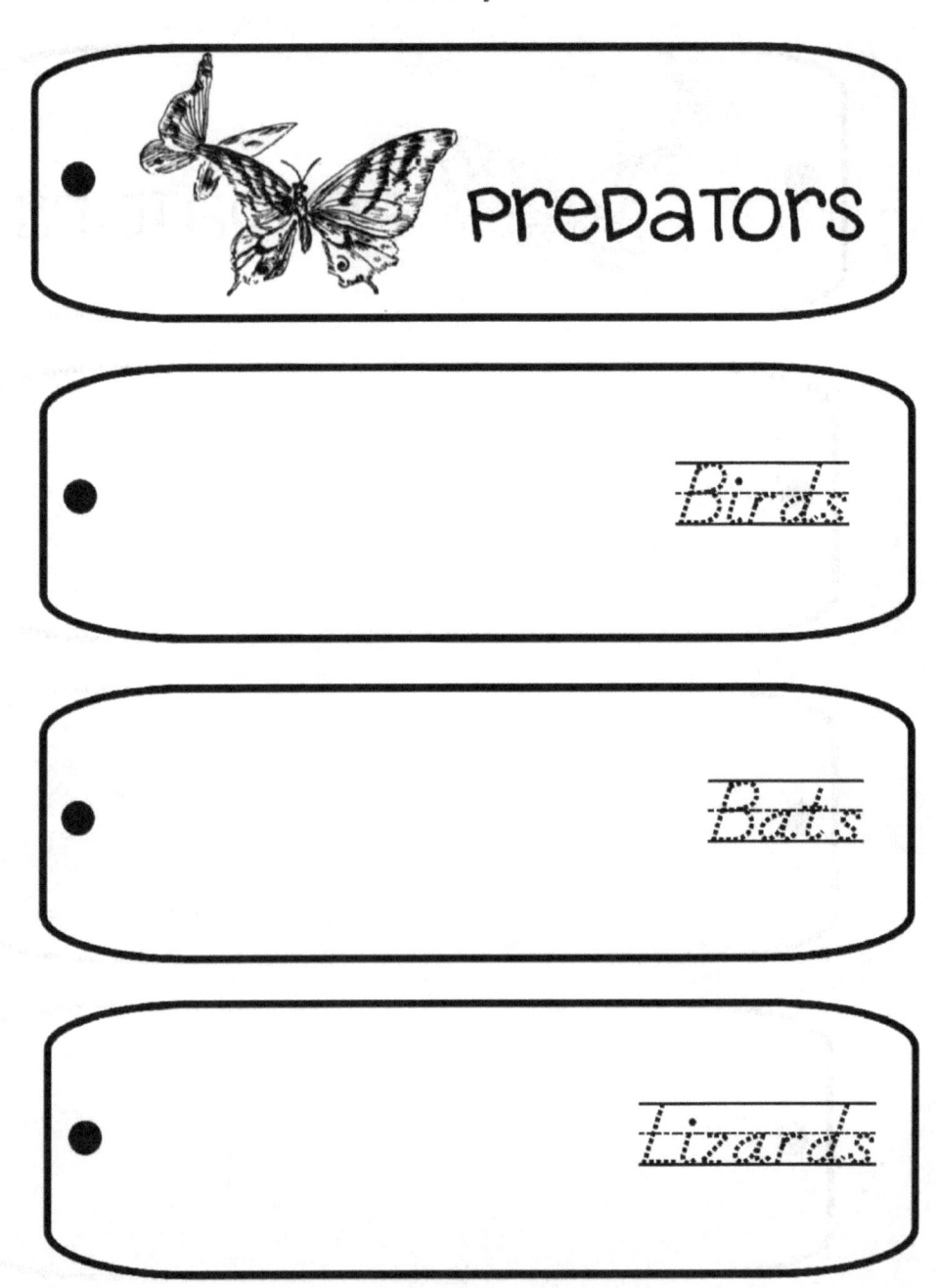

Activity 15

PREDATORS

Birds

Bats

Lizards

Activity 15

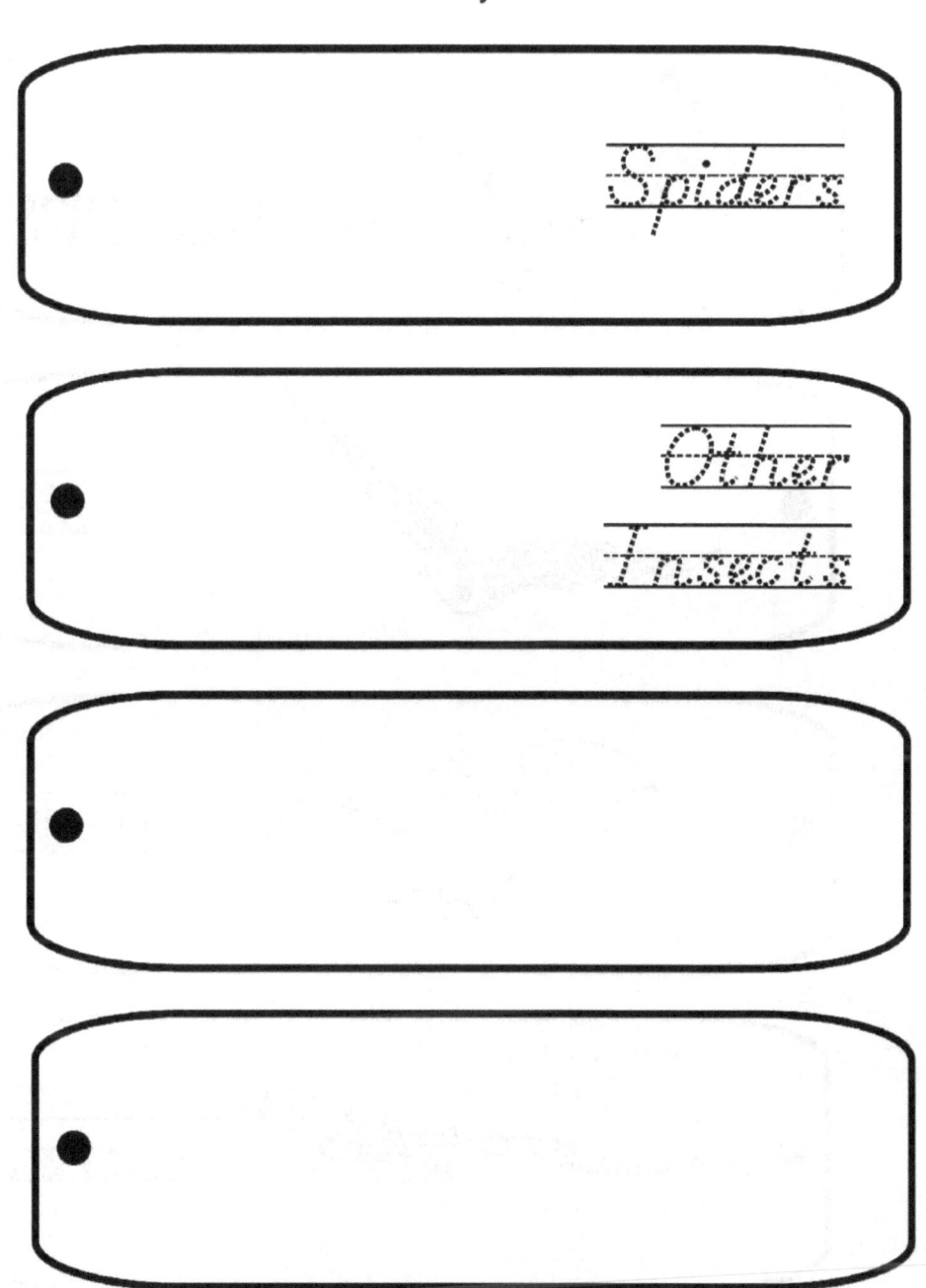

Spiders

Other Insects

Activity 15

PREDATORS

Birds

Bats

Lizards

68 | Page

Activity 15

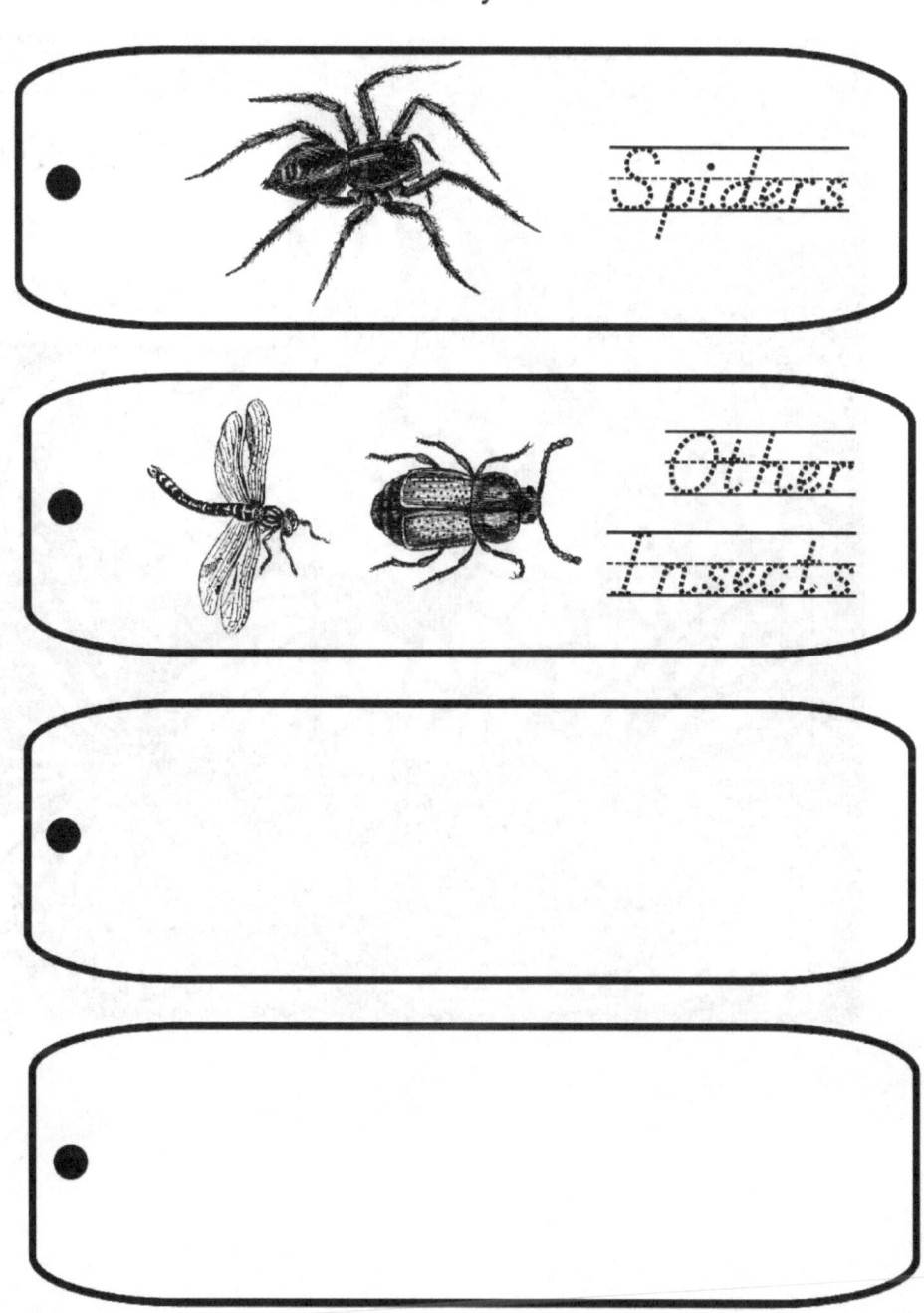

Spiders

Other
Insects

Activity 16

Activity 16

Camouflage

Poison

Flight

Activity 17

Methods for Surviving Cold Weather

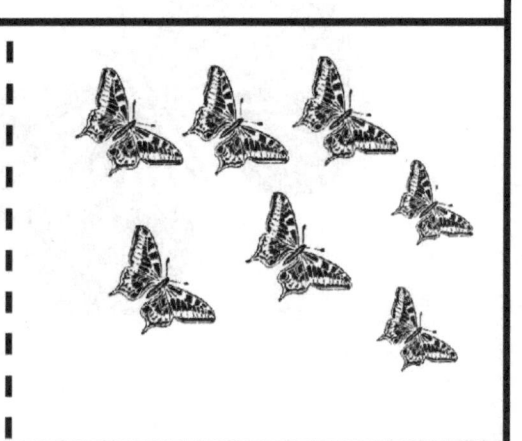

| Hibernation | Migration |

Activity 18

Migration Path

Activity 18

Paste into Info Card

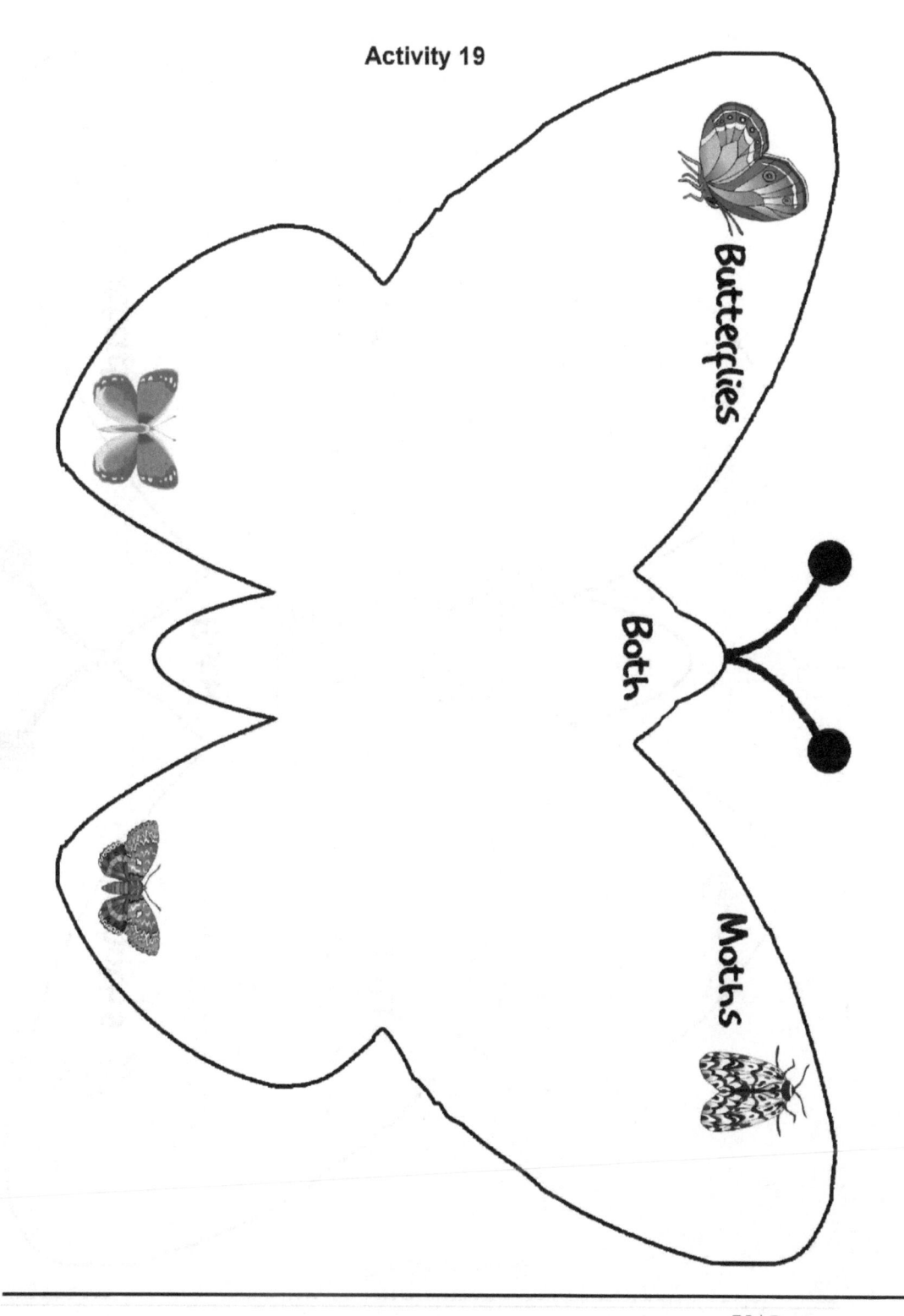

Activity 19

Butterflies

Both

Moths

75 | Page

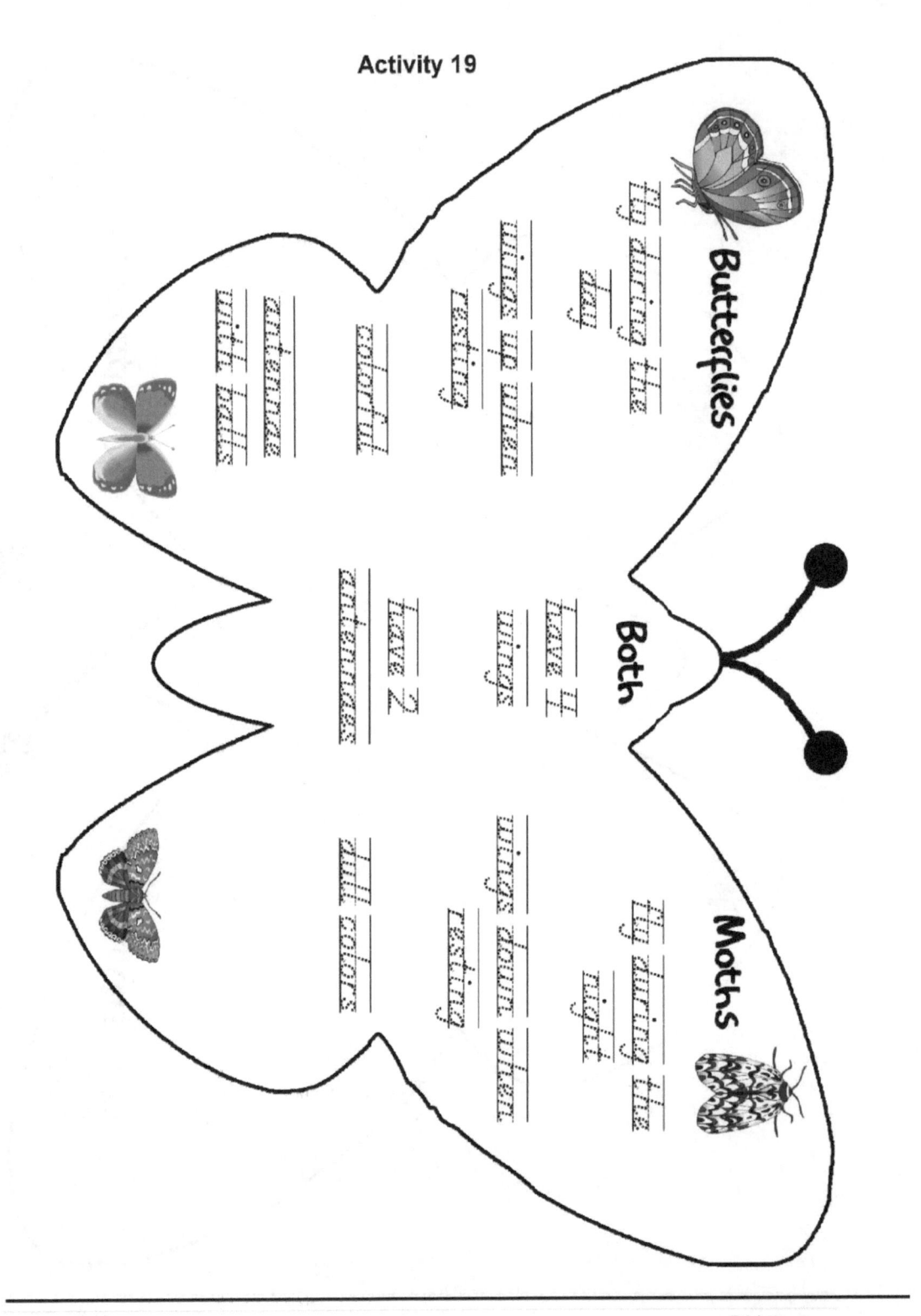

Activity 19

Butterflies
- fly during the day
- wings up when resting
- colorful
- thin antennae

Both
- have 4 wings
- have 2 antennae

Moths
- fly during the night
- wings down when resting
- dull colors

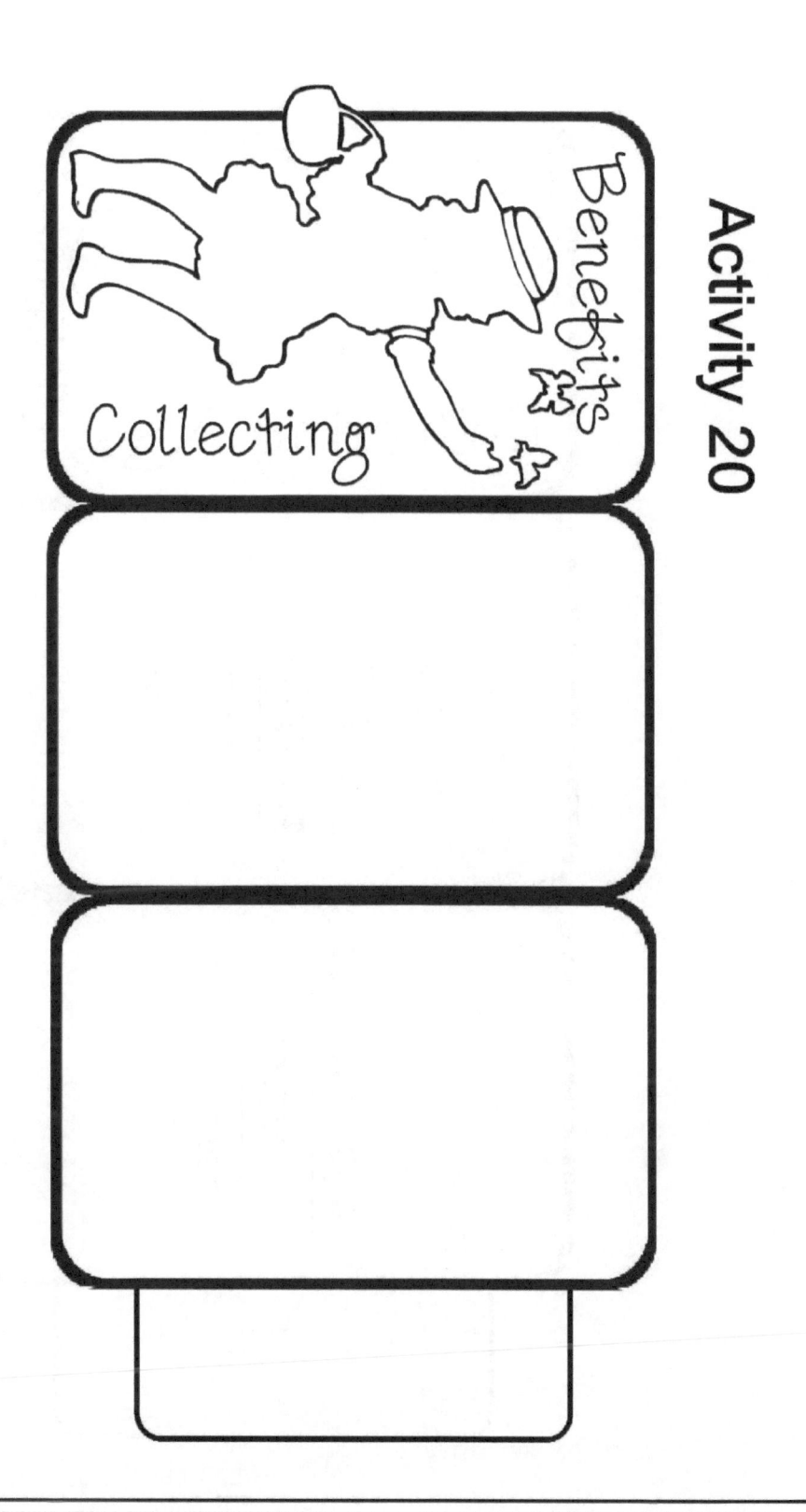

Activity 20

Benefits & Collecting

Activity 20

Collecting Benefits

stamps

fun

understand

scouting

feel

conservation

life

learn them

Activity 21

My Butterfly Garden

Activity 22

Activity 23

Butterfly Conservation

Activity 24

Answer Key

Activity 1: Vocabulary
Vocabulary: As you work through this unit, learn a few new vocabulary words each day. You do NOT have to learn every word in this unit; pick and choose the words you would like your student to learn.

Answer:
See Page 32

Activity 2: Butterfly Anatomy
Identify the parts of a butterfly.

Answer:
The parts colored and indicated should include:
Antennae
Compound eyes
Mouth
Thorax
Legs
Proboscis
Wings
Abdomen

For a younger child, you may need to help them locate the parts for the first few times. An older child may be able to do so on their own.

Activity 3: Proboscis Painting
Do you have a Proboscis?

Answer:
Project results will vary by student.

Activity 4: Compound Eyes
How does a butterfly see? Explain what compound eyes are.

Answer:
Results will vary by student. You may need to show your student how to draw one square at a time.

Activity 5: My Eyes
How do your eyes see?

Answer:
Answers will vary by student.

Activity 6: Exoskeletons
What is an exoskeleton?

Answer:
An exoskeleton is a hard outer shell on the outside of an insect. It protects the insect and acts like an outside skeleton.

Activity 7: Butterfly Habitats
List and describe the 3 main types of habitats that butterflies live in.

Answer:
Temperate – temperate butterflies are found in grasslands and woodlands. They need to be able to survive cold winters or migrate.
Mountains – mountain butterflies must be able to absorb and retain heat to survive cold temperatures and short summers.
Tropical – many very colorful butterflies live in tropical habitats where the weather is warm all year round.

Activity 8: Butterfly Diet
Describe a butterfly's diet.

Answer:
A butterfly's diet depends on its life cycle. Caterpillars eat leaves, seeds, pods or flowers. Some caterpillars also eat aphids and other caterpillars. Adult butterflies drink nectar from plants with their proboscis. Some butterflies also eat rotting fruit, tree sap, bird droppings, or animal dung. Many adult butterflies also drink liquid from wet sand or mud.

Activity 9: Drink Like a Butterfly
Drink like a butterfly!

Answer:
Answers will vary by student.

Activity 10: Pollination
Describe the sequence of pollination.

Answer:
1. A butterfly stops at a flower to drink nectar.
2. Tiny grains of pollen stick to its body.
3. It moves to another flower to drink.
4. The pollen grains slip off and pollinate the next flower.

Activity 11: Butterfly Life Cycle
Describe the life cycle of a butterfly.

Answer:
1. Egg sage
2. Caterpillar (larva)
3. Pupa (chrysalis)
4. Butterfly

Activity 12: Butterfly Eggs
How many eggs will hatch?

Answer:
Have the student color 2 squares. This is all the eggs that will survive!

Activity 13: My Cocoon
Make your own butterfly cocoon.

Answer:
Project results will vary by student.

Activity 14: My Butterfly Egg
Make your own butterfly egg!

Answer:
Project results will vary by student.

Activity 15: Predators
List the main predators of butterflies.

Answer:
Birds
Bats
Lizards
Spiders
Other Insects

Activity 16: Defense Mechanisms
What defense mechanisms do butterflies use to protect themselves?

Answer:
Camouflage
Poison
Flight

Activity 17: Baby, It's Cold Outside!
List two different ways that butterflies survive a cold winter climate.

Answer:
Hibernation – Some butterflies hibernate, which means that they lower their activity so much that they don't even eat. Butterflies hibernate in caves, hollow trees, under leaves, in sheds, or even inside houses.
Migration – Some butterflies migrate a short distance and others, like the monarch, migrate for hundreds or thousands of miles.

Activity 18: Butterfly Migration
Map the migration path of butterflies.

Answer:
You may wish to first help your student locate the migration path on a map or globe. Monarchs east of the Rockies often migrate to the coast of California and monarchs west of the Rockies often migrate to areas of northern Mexico.

Activity 19: Butterfly or Moth?
Compare a butterfly to a moth.

Answer:
Butterflies:
Fly during the day
Rest with their wings up and together
Often very colorful
Have little round balls at the end of their antennae

Both:
Belong to order Lepidopteron
Have similar bodies and wing structures

Moths:
Fly at night
Rest with their wings down and open
Often dull colors
Have fuzzy or feathery antennae with no round balls

Activity 20: Butterfly Collecting and Gardening
How does butterfly collecting and gardening help butterflies?

Answer:
Butterfly collecting can help butterflies if the collector writes down things like where the butterfly was found. This helps scientists understand more about a butterfly's habitat and how to protect them. Collectors can also raise butterflies from caterpillars in special netted habitats. Butterfly gardening can be helpful because the plants give butterflies the habitat and food that they need.

Activity 21: My Butterfly Garden
Design a butterfly garden. What flowers will you plant?

Answer:
Answers will vary by student and area that you live in, but may include:
Butterfly bush
Clover
Dogbane
Hollyhock
Lantana
Sassafras
Thistle
Verbena
Willow
Zinnia

Activity 22: Butterfly Info Card
Create an information card about a specific type of butterfly.

Answer:
Answers will vary based on ability level of student and butterfly chosen. Many species of butterflies are mentioned in the guide, or your student may have a favorite species they wish to learn more about.

Activity 23: Protecting the Butterflies
How can you help protect butterflies?

Answer:
We can help protect butterflies by planting gardens that have flowers that are helpful to butterflies and by making special places that will keep them safe. We can also raise butterflies and safely release them into the wild.

Activity 24: Butterfly Bookmark
Create a butterfly bookmark.

Answer:
Answers will vary by student. Be creati

Made in United States
Troutdale, OR
04/27/2025